RISING EAST: *The Journal of East London Studies*

Volume 2 *Number 1*

Rising East: The Journal of East London Studies is published three times a year by Lawrence & Wishart on behalf of the University of East London. The university acknowledges the generous contribution of the London East Training and Enterprise Council (LETEC) in co-funding this journal.

Design and Setting Art Services, Norwich

Subscriptions

For 1998, subscription rates are:

UK:	Individuals £20,	Institutions £50,
	Corporate Subscribers £100,	
Rest of the world:	Individuals £30,	Institutions £60,
	Corporate Subscribers £110.	

Single copies £10

All subscriptions administered by:

Lawrence & Wishart
99a Wallis Road, London E9 5LN
Tel: 0181 533 2506
Fax: 0181 533 7369

Contributions, correspondence and
books for review

Send to: Tim Butler, Editor, *Rising East: The Journal of East London Studies*, Department of Sociology, University of East London, Longbridge Road, Dagenham RM8 2AS.

Prospective writers are encouraged to contact the editors to discuss their ideas and to obtain a copy of our style sheet.

ISSN   1367 787X
ISBN   085315 8797

Printed in Great Britain by Cambridge University Press, Cambridge

The views expressed in this publication are solely those of the individual authors and do not represent in any way the official view of the University of East London or of London East Training and Enterprise Council

Contents

Volume 2: Number 1

Notes on Contributors

Tim Butler is Principal Lecturer in Sociology at the University of East London. He co-edited, with Mike Rustin, *Rising in the East? The regeneration of East London* (1996) and is author of *Gentrification and the Middle Classes* (1997).

Drew Stevenson is Chair of Urban Regeneration at University of East London. He was Head of Policy Planning at the GLC and has nearly thirty years' experience of London local government.

Mike Boulter is Professor of Palaebiology at the University of East London. He has described and interpreted many Cenozoic floras from the northern hemisphere and recently led a NATO workshop on Arctic climates.

Gavin Brown is an artist, activist and administrator. He lives in Stepney with his partner and grudgingly accepts that they are probably fairly typical gay gentrifiers.

Phil Cohen is Reader in Cultural Studies where he directs the Centre for New Ethnicities Research. His most recent publications are *Rethinking the Youth Question* (1997) and *Island Stories* (1997).

Darren Simmonds works as the Human Resources Analyst for London East TEC. Previously he was with the Isle of Wight TEC.

Sarah Monks is a Research Fellow at the National Maritime Museum, Greenwich. She is curating a forthcoming exhibition of the museum's art collections as part of its £20 million Neptune Court Project, opening in April 1999.

Rehan Jamil is a photographer who lives and works in Tower Hamlets.

Richard McKeever works at the Centre for New Ethnicities Research where he is the Projects and Development Officer.

Debjani Chatterjee is a poet, writer and storyteller. She chairs the Arts Council's Translation Advisory Group and is a founder-member of South Yorkshire's Bengali Women's Support Group. Her most recent book is *A Little Bridge* (1997).

Vikki Rix is a Research Fellow in the Department of Sociology at the University of East London.

Action as an antidote to fear of failure

This issue of *Rising East* appears close to the first anniversary of the first Labour government for twenty years. Inevitably, expectations were running higher for much of 1997 than the capability of any government to deliver - although by the beginning of 1998 questions were being asked about the will to deliver on social inequality. What can we reasonably expect from a Labour government? The question of inequality has become increasingly complicated, particularly now that we now are beginning to understand the ecological consequences of continued economic growth. No longer can anti-poverty measures be finessed within some formulation about the benefits of economic growth.

We live, and look set to continue to live, in a capitalist world; that does not however necessarily mean those who come from poor families or poor areas, or poor families in poor areas, need automatically be consigned to a life of poverty and deprivation. This surely is the challenge for New Labour, just like it was for Old Labour in 1945. Equality of opportunity however has sociological implications for New Labour which mean that it hits hard at middle-class privilege, which has become New Labour's electoral bastion.

Tony Blair's assumption appears to be that globalisation is a fact and there is little that we can do to challenge its economic and social inexorability. Forming a strong Europe with a committed European programme is probably the most effective way of channeling contemporary tendencies towards economic globalisation. Unfortunately the Labour government has decided that this is not a time for leadership around the most important symbol of Europe's challenge to globalisation: economic and monetary union. It prefers to wait and see, which Britain might have done after Munich but luckily for the rest of us decided not to.

, Roy Hattersley claims that Harold Wilson in the 1960s had the courage to face down the Governor of the Bank of England over his demands that the Government overturn its manifesto pledges on the economy. Tony Blair appears unprepared to take on an ex-motorbike dealer over the issue of banning tobacco advertising when faced with the threat that Britain's niche engineering business in racing cars might move abroad. So far so bad: even if you accept the argument that there is nothing you can do about a globalised economy, one might have thought that challenging the right of a tobacco industry in disarray to go on killing yet more people each year would be indicative of what a modern government might do to support citizens in what has been termed 'risk society'. He could even have hidden behind Europe but chose not to. Bernie Ecclestone, however, might yet prove to be a Rubicon for Tony Blair.

The rest of us should also learn the lesson from this debacle which is that governments are no longer in a position to determine but they are in a position to influence. Britain could have hoped to have influenced the debate in Europe and Britain over economic and monetary union, over smoking and indeed over food safety. On all three it has chosen not to because the risks of being on the wrong side were perceived as too great. This, it seems to me, is the problem of modern politics: an inability to take risks and thus face the possibility of losing. The greatest innovation perhaps of the 1980s, and particular of Majorism, was the development of the concept of 'blame management' - far worse to have tried and been wrong than to have done nothing. It is this legacy which we now face and in a sense we have the first government that is wedded to permanent popularity - we are, as it were, in a situation of a permanent election. We need to learn the lesson of this in our attempts to influence the policy process.

The Government might be right or it might be wrong on welfare reforms and the prioritisation of health and education, but it seems that it is determined to do nothing that will make it unpopular - hard choices come second. This probably means that nothing radical in a progressive sense will be done: simply because being unpopular with the middle classes means losing votes, whilst doing nothing for those with very little has almost zero political cost. Leadership is about influencing events and persuading people that your policy or programme is better than anybody else's. Sometimes you lose but the history of the last fifty years, with one notable exception, would appear to be that we should do nothing that might upset those who own the economy. That exception was the Labour government of 1945-51 which, despite its mistakes, managed to drive through a programme of radical social and economic reform. It made huge demands on the British working class (and most of the relatively tiny middle class) in order to rebuild an essentially national capitalist economy - most of the international bits had been given to the US in return for 50 clapped out destroyers. It is now widely accepted that Attlee succeeded in achieving what he set out to do, and took people with him: the popular vote of the Labour Party in 1951 was the highest ever and the fact that Labour lost the election had more to do with the vagaries of the electoral system than the popularity of the Tories. There is a lesson in all of this for Tony Blair which one suspects he may not want to hear, but it is that in the same way that the working classes of the 1940s were prepared to make sacrifices for social progress, so today's very different middle classes might be prepared to pay taxes for genuine social gain.

A modern class politics

Although by no means the first public school educated leader of the Labour Party, Tony Blair combines his background with a lack of loyalty to class politics - not necessarily an outmoded version of working-class politics but a modern-class politics. I think it is interesting that nobody blinks when confronted with the earnings of the spouse of the Labour leader and those of many of his colleagues in the cabinet and party. A lawyer earning several hundred thousand a year is not a problem for New Labour or the electorate in the way that a manager or entrepreneur would be (Geoffrey Robinson, please note). However, such people do not have the detachment of the Tory grandees for whom politics was a duty which rarely impacted on their personal lives, nor even of most of the parvenus of the Thatcher and Major cabinets who insulated themselves from the consequences of their actions through private education for the kids and private medical insurance for themselves. This is not something even the most brazen New Labour politician can do. For this generation of politicians, politics is about minimising risk in an increasingly risky world and, to some extent at least, that means sharing the risk, and it really is only the state that can do this, particularly as genetic screening and other techniques mean that private insurance schemes will discriminate between individuals - however wealthy.

Politics has become a vocation, or a career just like being a lawyer where you argue your case and then go home. However just as it is bad business for a lawyer to lose too many cases, so it is for a politician: failure has direct career implications and although there are generous early retirement schemes, one does not resign nor does one want to become unpopular with the managers of Britain's media. What this means is that we have to build the commitment to a radical social programme into the job description of the new Labour government and show that a radical social programme is something that, whilst all may not benefit from all of the time, they are very happy that others are able to - because there 'for the grace of god go I'. In other words, just as many male managers have been forced to take issues of gender (and to a lesser extent ethnicity) seriously so we have to ensure that poverty does not become something the boys joke about in the gents - whilst Harriet takes the flak.

The problem however is a real one: how does one improve the lot of the bottom 30 per cent of the population? Blair surely is right to distinguish between welfare and work, and we should not create a dependency culture, but equally nothing is to be gained by a form of social 'cold turkey'. What rights do people have to influence the policy process? I have some difficulty envisaging Tony Blair coming down to East London and taking his jacket off and rolling up his sleeves, yet if the problem cannot be solved here it cannot be solved anywhere - precisely because the complexity of modern day deprivation is the norm rather than the exception. In each editorial of *Rising East* I have reiterated the litany of East London's multiple deprivations: quite simply it is poor and deprived and deserves better. Quite rightly, it has high expectations of the new Labour government but after a year it might ask how realistic these expectations might be. We would however be wrong to write off the government's attempts to grapple with these problems: we need to be brutally realistic about the continued need to shame the government into keeping the poverty issue at the top of its agenda. But this does not mean that we should not be open to its project of guaranteeing the health and education of the whole population.

Public investment on the agenda

Nobody voted Labour with illusions. The Labour Party made it very clear that its goals were limited, that it regarded its hands tied economically and that there would be no quick fixes but that it would do something about getting people to work, it would do something about the issue of governance and it would do its best to prioritise health and education. There is some evidence that it has stuck to those priorities. We now have a Green Paper which is about the kind of governance that London should have, the 'welfare to work' scheme is now up and running and there is a high degree of realism about the problems involved in getting the long-term unemployed into training and into work and real efforts appear to be being made to tackle the problems of education from the bottom up. We have covered all of these issues in this journal (with the exception of health which is a major issue in East London and shall be tackled in future issues of the journal). What I think *Rising East* has shown is that what we need are ideas and partners to take these ideas forward with and optimism about our ability to make things better: fear of failure should not be an issue because if we are frightened of getting things wrong then we will do nothing. The Government, despite its mistakes and its tendency to arrogance and stasis, is not shut off from ideas and to demands being put on it in its key priority areas. We need to start thinking about how these key areas - particularly those of education and health - can be delivered in ways that are effective and progressive. Most of the 1980s were devoted to defending the institutions of the welfare state and most of the running was made by the ideologues - and not just those on the right - who used arguments for cost efficiency to impose their models of a mass provision which in almost every arena, from the BBC to the primary school, involved an intellectual 'dumbing down'. What we are now witnessing are the costs of this. The time has come to think about the content of public services and public investment. *Rising East* has already begun to inform and stimulate such a debate - what Michael Rustin in our second issue referred to as a 'conversation', an example of which might be Greg Clarke's suggestion, in the same publication, that we might use some of the regeneration tools developed in the USA. Another would be the radical implications that might be drawn from Phil Cohen's article, in the third number, about the role higher education might play in relation to East London's fractured communities.

There is one other fact and that is that we do live in a different world from the one that today's decision-makers grew up in. Whilst I might disagree with the Government's view that globalisation is a given and that therefore there is nothing we can do about it or its implications, I do not believe that today's society has much in common with that inherited by the Attlee government in 1945. They are both capitalist but that is about it. Today we are increasingly living in an economy, especially in London, that is dominated by flows of information (as opposed to stocks of physical assets) where economic decisions are taken across global space in real time. Neither states, governments nor corporations, however large, have individual or collective control over this economy. The constituencies have changed, class and the nation state have little bearing on individual or collective identity whereas those of nation, ethnicity, gender have an increasing power;[1] if economic power is concentrated in the control of information and social power is concentrated in networks, then as I argued in the editorial to the previous issue, the long-term goal for East London must be to 'open itself up' so that its people can participate and benefit in and from those networks rather than being closed off from them. Realistically, this means that we should concentrate on giving its people access to the London economy rather than falling back into the kind of autarchic economic regeneration programme that has tried to bring the jobs to East London for generations. The history of that has been very apparent: for the most part the jobs have been low paid, physically demanding and intellectual drudgery.

Of course, once East Londoners compete on an equal footing with those from elsewhere in the London region, then East London becomes a good place to invest and all of its historical disadvantages become sources of comparative advantage. That does require that we have a fifteen year social regeneration programme in which education and support for vulnerable families is central. If Jack Straw is finding it difficult to 'touch base' with William in a family with an income of well over £100,000 a year, imagine the problems of a single parent on a tenth of that amount. Of course it is about 'quality time' (plus a sensible policy on drugs that is not trying to recreate what the US learned didn't work sixty years ago), but you don't have to be unreconstructed old Labour to argue that when you are poor there is very little 'quality' or 'time'. 'Poor but honest' worked in the fevered brows of Victorian misanthropes but what it actually gave us was the welfare state because the alternative was too awful to contemplate - haven't we learnt anything in the last 100 years?

This issue

In this issue we cover a number of the subjects to which I have already referred. We lead with an extensive article on the Green Paper on the Governance of London. It is drafted by Drew Stevenson but represents the view of those working on East London at the University of East London. It is a radical contribution in the way that it recognises the obvious advantages of an elected authority and mayor to 'get things done', yet at the same time it argues that this should be extended to improve representation not just of the electors living in London but also of those organisations, particularly the voluntary sector, that play such a vital part in the life of the capital and are not currently recognised in its governance. We would welcome further articles in this crucial area.

Greg Smith's article 'A very social capital' is an attempt to draw on the academic literature on social capital and apply it to East London. The relevance of this is beyond question, particularly given the problems with economic capital and its disengagement with the area, but Greg shows that there are considerable grounds for pessimism about the involvement of local populations in what might be termed civil society. Mike Boulter, who is Professor of Palaebiology at the University of East London and an internationally respected figure in telling us about what happened millions of years ago, might seem a rather strange contributor to a journal essentially concerned with the regeneration of the sub region. I hope though that others will find his article as fascinating as I did, not just in terms of understanding the ground that we walk over every day but also for the context in which he places current concerns about climate change: as he says, this is not the first time the globe's climate has changed but it does seem to be the first time it has happened as a result of human agency.

Much is made about the cultural diversity of East London and how this is one of the area's major strengths. Gavin Brown's article on the gay population of Tower Hamlets is a major contribution in beginning to understand the nature of that diversity rather than just proclaiming it. He shows how Tower Hamlets has developed as a major centre of gay residence and looks at some of the implications of this for the borough and for East London more generally. Coming after the article by John Eade and Chris Mele in the last issue, which compared the east sides of New York and London, we are beginning to develop an analysis of some of possibilities that are now taking place in the borough. This is further added to by the interview in this issue with Michael Keith, currently leader of Tower Hamlets council, which gives an insight into the thinking underlying the council's support for the 'Rich Mix' project. He also talks about the Green Paper and the role of the government which hopefully will add a further dimension both to this editorial and to the UEL paper on the governance of London.

Finally, Darren Simmonds who works in the research team at the London East Training and Enterprise Council (LETEC) provides an extremely useful briefing on 'welfare to work' which builds on the article in the last issue by Stephen Timms. Not only does he explain how the scheme is intended to work but shows how it will operate on the ground in East London. He also highlights where some of the potential problems might occur in its implementation which will have to be dealt with if this flagship scheme is to meet its ambitious, and socially vital, goals.

Vikki Rix's work, published here as 'Demography, Family Diversity and Changing Household Structures throughout London East', is not only ground-breaking in mapping and analysing the massive demographic shifts in the sub region, but she also points up the shortcomings in a government policy which threatens to penalise the most vulnerable in society as the 'welfare to work' regime begins to bite in a part of London where jobs are hard to find.

Artyfacts leads with a vivid account of the role Greenwich played as a tourist spectacle to an eighteenth and nineteenth century English public. Sarah Monks demonstrates that the flimsy Millennium Dome is an unworthy successor to the splendour of the Greenwich Hospital, and that in the

Greenwich Pensioner even Peter Mandelson would have met his match! *Rising East* is pleased to showcase new photographic talent in the series of photos by young Tower Hamlets' photographer Rehan Jamil. His images of different generations of Bangladeshi men in Whitechapel emphasise the staying power of one of London East's most dynamic communities. Jack London was one of the most imaginative of Victorian urban explorers and in a thought-provoking piece edited by Richard McKeever, two photographers who have been working with pupils form Morpeth School in Bethnal Green assess the value of his legacy for a new generation of young East Londoners. In Syed Manzurul Islam, Bengali residents in East London have a brilliant storyteller to speak their stories. His first collection of short stories, *The Mapmakers of Spitalfields*, is considered by Debjani Chatterjee in our final section.

Tim Butler

1. Many will recognise these claims as being a simplification of the ideas being argued for by Manuel Castells in his recent trilogy *The Information Age: Economy, Society and Culture (1996-97)*, Oxford: Blackwell.

New leadership for London

London's governance

Drew Stevenson

Drew Stevenson welcomes the Government's commitment to establish regional government for London. He argues that concepts of government are now overlapped by those of governance, that the societal framework defining the future of governance is changing rapidly and that the role of sub regions within London is the key emerging issue.

It is no coincidence that the introduction of regional tiers of government is currently either taking place or being discussed widely in Europe and beyond. Even within the confines of the UK, the Government is introducing a new tier of government in Scotland and Wales at the same time as London's governance is discussed. Similarly, discussion is taking place on the introduction of regional government across the country. Whilst there are some common issues to be faced (for example, subsidiary in the context of the EU), London is a special case. This is partly due to the 'democratic deficit' that exists in London and the need to re-establish democratic systems in London which others already have. Second, the relationship between the government of London and national government has been a long and complex one with questions of political power and access to resources being at the core of that relationship. They remain there today.

They are given a new slant, however, by the creation of a directly elected mayor - someone who will be 'the voice of London'. This heightens the need to look carefully at the relationships between real and perceived authority, access to the needs of London versus the rest of the UK, and democratic accessibility. To introduce a new tier that gave the appearance of authority whilst in fact being ineffectual would not only be bad for London, but would be a further blow to the dwindling interest in local government generally. Conversely any central government will be cautious about the amount of power it cedes to the governance of a large capital and world class city.

It will be hard to get the balance right and almost impossible to do so in one move. The need for flexibility, review and a transparent analysis of the real issues both now and over time will be essential. In drafting this submission we tried to avoid being dogmatic about issues where clearly more than one valid approach can be taken.[1] Because of the structure of the document however, in which we try to establish a set of principles which help to frame a consistent set of answers, there are many areas on which we do have a clear view. Where doubt remains, we have on occasion explored more than one option, and we will be interested in continuing the debate over the further stages, through the White Paper, Referendum, Bill and Committee stages.

THE APPROACH

When considering all of the options for London governance and all of the detail, it is easy to lose sight of the fundamental issue. At stake is the creation of a new regional tier of governmental competence for one of the three great World Cities amid the excitement and changing aspirations created by the birth of a new millennium.

How the Government goes about it, and what the eventual outcomes are, should become role models of good governance for major cities around the world. For a brief moment, the absence of an existing tier of regional government in London is an advantage; we are not tied to existing custom, we can take a step back and decide what is needed and what is appropriate for London.

London needs government that is relevant not only to itself as a place, but is relevant to the changing wider governmental context, relevant to its time, and relevant to the spirit of the age. It needs a new model - one based on the fitness of its purpose for the future, not the past, and one that captures the imagination, confidence and whole-hearted support of London's people, businesses and institutions. Without these, London governance will rapidly become ineffectual, since we live in an age where people do not for long tolerate that which is irrelevant to them, is isolated from them or which ignores their interests.

We believe that the creation of a new model will be framed by certain key factors.

i) Macro contextual changes. The impact of globalisation, the gradual emergence (notwithstanding some hot spots) of a less divided world order, the strengthening of the European Union, combined with decentralisation within the UK, the spatial concentration of powerful economic sectors related to new information and knowledge-based technologies, are likely to have a slow but radical effect on the relative importance and required strengths of different tiers of government.

There is, currently, a disorienting shift of power from the national

London's governance

level upwards and downwards. The nation state isn't disappearing, but it is undergoing radical change. There is also a profound, though less visible, effect at the local level. Local government now has to deal with the economic, cultural and social consequences of actions and trends which are transnational to a greater degree than ever before. The means of response, therefore, are increasingly less easily grasped in one locality by purely local action.

In essence, we are likely to see a continuing growth of *supra or cross nation state unions*, the consequent weakening of the role of the *nation state*, squeezed also by the rise in economic importance and clearer functional roles of *the regions*. Within the largest and most powerful regions (viz. Greater London) the sheer complexity and diversity will lead to the growing importance of *sub regions* within the region. *Local government* may be diversified further and eventually replaced with the creation of a tier somewhere between the current boroughs (in the London situation) and the equivalent of communes, emerging in response to demands for real and visible control over that which is needed day by day at the local level, and the recognition that many economic issues can only be resolved over a wider area.

It could be argued that the other major contemporary world-wide paradigms - concern for the environment, or green issues, evolving into concepts of sustainability in a wider sense - will reinforce the emergence of such a new order, since many aspects of these can only be tackled in a city-wide or sub-regional context - for example transport, waste disposal, recycling and energy.

ii) Globalisation. Ironically, within the pressure to conform to the needs of the global economy and information society, there is an equal pressure that emphasises the importance of place and the role of difference. Again, this focus is at a regional or sub-regional scale, not national or local. This will affect not just the need to reassess the specific economic attractions of city states, regions and sub regions but, in consequence, realign the strengths and functions of different tiers of government, to review the demands that a 24 hour information society puts upon the city and hence its government, and the impact of information technology on the function of government itself (see below).

iii) Societal relationships. Government cannot, even if it wished, remain aloof from the marked changes in relationships that have swept powerfully across the UK in the past 30 years. This change has been described as a shift in relationships that were based in the years after the war, on a model of *dependence (the welfare state)* to those based on *independence (the Thatcher years)* to the emergent model of *interdependence*. To illustrate these new relationships one only has to think of concepts of stakeholding, or the creation of interdependent 'just in time' delivery models. Similarly one could point to the current emphasis on the role of partnerships. They are not new ways of working based on coincidence or fashion. They are the reflection of deep-seated changes that are running through society, recreating it in new forms. There is no sign that such developments are on the wane. On the contrary they are likely to grow and have fundamental implications for the effective and relevant governance of London.

iv) Norms and Values. These changes are also mirrored at the individual level by the breakdown of certain rules of organisation and control. Within the past ten years we have witnessed the virtual disappearance of people's trust in institutions and in authority and we have seen the complete loss of deference as a way of ordering society. The drop in voter-interest in elections is not an isolated issue, it is part of this broader change in norms. It will not be amenable to simple solutions, but can be addressed by aligning governance more with the new reality of the ways in which people think and act. We are seeing the birth of a society that is less easy to order, less compliant and more questioning; a society where people want less control by others over their lives. There are, again, clear implications for styles of government.

Alongside this there has been a gradual but long running and deep-seated *shift in values*. Longitudinal surveys in the UK have shown that people tend to form their values between the ages of about 17 and 24 and then carry them throughout life. Of course they change at the margins, but not significantly. The way in which values *do* change over time lies in the *difference between values held by succeeding generations*, thus, for example, the values held by young people today are very different from those held by people who were born between the wars. They had different values when they were young and they retain those different values today.

The shift over time has been, broadly speaking, away from values associated with the need for shelter, stability and survival and the consequent need for authority and control, to values based more on integration, emotion, ease and green issues - which are transforming lifestyles and ideas as well as expectations about the future - and notions about relevant governance in the future; see for example the work by DEMOS submitted to the 'London Study'.[4]

v) Sense of community. The very notion of community and its relevance to local government is also undergoing significant change. In essence notions of community, based on neighbourhood or location, have been considerably weakened to be replaced in part by communities of interest and/or identity which may or may not correspond to any geographical boundary. There are both positive and negative implications for regional and local governance.

vi) Information technology. We are in the middle of an 'information revolution'. Information and communications technologies [ICTs] are changing organisational and social life - and therefore political life. It is now possible to offer citizens a vast array of on-line information about the activities of government at all levels. It is also possible to offer opportunities for comment and consultation, and thus for input to decision-making, on a mass basis. If the Government's plans for penetration of ICTs into all kinds of educational institution, libraries and other public centres are realised, then these may well be the polling stations of the future - in addition, of course, to the home.

Whilst informal democracies can and will alter swiftly and formal democracy will increasingly be subject to pressures to change, there are major questions as to who will, in practice, have access to the technology. Equally, whilst the dynamics of the relationships between individual citizens, organisations, interest groups and elected representatives will alter dramatically, they will raise issues for the power and leadership required of the mayor and authority. An authority run on a series of referenda would rapidly sink to short term populism and lack the ability to take the hard decisions in the longer term interest.

vii) Ideology. Notions of what government is actually for have changed, not just because of the factors listed above, but in the affirmation of a powerful ideological stance which reached its height in the UK in the 1980s. It was, at least in part, a creature of its time - with the approaching collapse of communist regimes in Europe and beyond - but one which arguably has now been subsumed and recreated by the strength of the forces listed above. For example, the ideologically motivated introduction of compulsory competitive tendering and the destruction of the notion of local government as the sole local provider of services under the wing of the welfare state, has been transformed by the embrace of local government (albeit unevenly) of concepts of customer care, of choice, and a less patronising and arrogant provision of arms length services.

This list of factors which will frame the reality of governance in London could be expanded - the ageing population, the rise of fundamentalism, revision of liberalism etc. - but we argue that the seven factors above are paramount.

So what are the implications for the future governance of London when considering its nature, form and functions, as well as its 'style'? We believe it is possible to draw up a set of principles from this analysis which will help to ensure a relevant and consistent approach. But before setting those out, we look briefly at London itself so that the principles are specific to London rather than merely relating to wider questions of good governance.

WHAT KIND OF LONDON?

This is not the place to go into detail on some of the long term trends that are shaping London's future, nor is it yet possible to form a clear vision of what kind of London might be considered desirable and appropriate for the future. These issues are currently being addressed in the 'London Study' led by the Association of London Government with significant funding from the European Commission and a range of partners.

However, some early, albeit tentative, conclusions can be drawn. We concentrate on those which appear to have a direct bearing on the kind of governance that will be needed in London and the principles that should underlie it.

The study is not alone in stressing the importance of multicultural London; indeed some have gone so far as to say that the strength and depth of multiculturalism in London will become its strongest asset in a globalised world. One fifth of Londoners are from the ethnic minorities. In ten years, it is predicted that this will become one third. Within East London, in the London Borough of Newham, there is no 'majority community'. In this context, the very term ethnic minority begins to become meaningless. London is becoming cosmopolitan on an entirely new scale, in ways which are in register with its 'world city' status. It will have world-wide ties of family and culture, as well as global economic and communications links. It will be far more than just the capital city of the United Kingdom and its government.

Some other themes can be identified:

- The need to define and support specific sectors within the capital as a whole and within the sub regions.
- The need to match action on social exclusion with actions on economic competitiveness and inward investment.
- The need to define and achieve sustainability in economic, social and environmental terms.
- The need to build on a tradition of innovation.
- The need to support and develop cultural industries.
- The need to harness cross-sectoral commitment to implement common objectives and to strengthen existing partnerships.
- The need to protect the best that London has to offer, to develop it in sustainable ways and to widen access.
- The need to understand the complementarity of the major sub regions within London.

London's governance

Whilst many of these notions remain, as yet, at the level of general concepts, they point in a particular direction which is also in tune with the analysis we have given above in terms of changing societal relationships and so on. They have similar implications not so much for good governance as for relevant and sustainable governance for London.

In light of our analysis of the factors affecting governance generally and the specific case of London, we now turn to the question of principles.

A set of guiding principles

First, we need to distinguish between London government and London's governance. The former we define as a set of democratic arrangements which exercise particular responsibilities and powers, set budgets, make policies, implement strategies (in partnership), hold assets and employ staff in fulfilment of the role of being the Greater London Authority. Government can be statutorily prescribed and standards set for performance.

London's governance we define as the web or network of relationships between local, regional, national and European tiers of government impacting on London life and between these tiers and the multiplicity of bodies and agencies which deliver services, form partnerships, undertake developments, and help formulate policies, plans and strategies for London. Governance cannot be prescribed, but is achieved, for example, by the quality of goal-sharing, goodwill, co-operation and information exchange which the participants can sustain. The principles on which government is founded go a long way towards determining how far governance can be successful.

If it is to create leadership and act within a London-wide picture of the capital's condition and needs, London government must be devised so it can tackle deficiencies, create alignments of strategic interests and move to a sustainable future.

This leads us to *a set of guiding principles* for good governance relevant to London, as follows:

- *A strong tier of regional government is vital,* not just to the competitive success of the region in a global economy, but for the economic and political health of the nation.
- *The role and importance of this tier will grow over time* as that of the nation state shifts.
- *This leads to the need for flexibility within continuity* and the need to deal transparently with issues of political power and access to resources.

- *The growth of inter-dependence* as a way of ordering society will fundamentally affect the role, structure, shape and accountability streams of London government. The role of partnership will lie at the core of effective institutions.

- *Changes in values and the demise of deference* mean that whilst people will increasingly tolerate the differing lifestyles of individuals, notwithstanding the rise of fundamentalism in some sections of the community, they will not tolerate the arbitrary or irrelevant use of power, nor abide its abuse, corruption or sleaze. Systems based purely on command and control will become inoperable.

- *All sectors will demand both a say in government and demonstrable public accountability;* concepts of the public accountability of private bodies which are active in cross sectoral partnerships will need to be developed.

- *The growth of communities of interest and identity* will provide more powerful checks on the arbitrary exercise of power (particularly at the regional level) than spatial communities ever could.

- *Information technology* will create realisable demands for more involvement in government and public accountability; it will enable more accurate analysis of radical options whilst heightening tensions between short-term populism and longer term leadership.

- *Last, but not least, there is an emerging set of beliefs, short of an ideology, about what government needs to be for in the coming decade.* It is certainly not top-down, nor about the direct provision of services in all areas; it is not primarily about regulating and controlling, nor even about co-ordinating. It is more about facilitating, harnessing and innovating, about encouraging autonomy within a framework of democratic accountability, about partnership, about shared strategies based on effective analysis, competence and the clear definition of desirable outcomes in the real world, about making a difference, about additionality, subsidiarity and transparency and about public scrutiny, relevance and review. And it needs to do all this not just to promote economic competitiveness, but to deal with social exclusion, promoting inclusion and improving the quality of life.

The construction of a new tier of government in London, and the partnerships and means of access to resources it will rely upon to implement its vision, need to go with the grain of these principles. London government needs to be given reserve powers to enable it to do what it needs to do, but be given no powers that it does not need to exercise its functions.

Some might argue that whereas these principles are desirable aspirations, in 'the real world' they are not achievable. We would argue the reverse - that is to say that unless these principles genuinely underpin the new tier of government, whilst it may be initially established, it will not be sustainable. The clear message coming through from the changes that we have described, as well as from the practical political experience across Europe in particular over the past decade, is that where notions and practices of government are too far out of step with the 'spirit of the times' then governments crumble. The implications of such a collapse in the new government of London, both for the capital and the country, would be drastic. The process and practice must be informed by up to date principles of good governance.

Within the context of these principles, we now turn to issues of form, structure and function.

The structure and function of London governance

The debate about the Greater London Authority has tended to be more focused on structure than function. This has largely been driven by the stated commitment to a directly elected mayor. If that is accepted as a given, as it is in this paper, it has fundamental implications for the structure of the GLA and the need to encompass a wide range of competencies and functions which will change over time. It is those issues to which we now turn in light of the principles set out above.

First we describe briefly the totality of the structure of London-wide governance as we see it, and then consider each of the three basic components in more detail. The three elements are the directly elected mayor and constituency members of a Greater London Authority, a cross sector Greater London Assembly, and a series of cross sector implementing agencies. Within this structure we are proposing a different view to that put forward in the Green Paper.

The mayor and the Greater London Authority would be directly elected and comprise the mayor together with about 40 members elected on a constituency basis. Together they would form the democratically elected and accountable executive arm of London-wide government. The mayor, although directly elected, would also be the titular head of the authority and work with a number of commissioners from amongst the members of the authority to assist his/ her office and would further employ a small core of officers. Amongst a number of functions, set out in more detail below, the two most critical for the mayor's office and the authority would be the development of a shared vision for the future of London and then the successful implementation of that vision. In neither arena should the authority act alone. In both it needs to act with others and be seen to be publicly accountable.

The Greater London Assembly would meet one half of this need. We propose that the mayor, representing the democratically elected authority, reports to a cross sectoral Greater London Assembly whose members are themselves elected from electoral colleges in order to give maximum transparency to this tier. The principal and statutory roles of the assembly would be to act as a partner in the development and ownership of the vision, and as a scrutiny body regarding budgets, performance and implementation. The assembly would be able to enforce public debate and provide an input from its wider perspective, but not ultimately to block the ability of the elected mayor and authority to act.

A series of agencies, such as the London Development Agency, would complete the picture. They would be formally created primarily for the purposes of developing strategy in their areas of competence in the context of the London-wide vision and ensuring implementation. The agencies could vary in form, and would change in number over time, but they would essentially be cross sectoral, each reporting annually to the authority via a commissioner appointed for that purpose.

In short, there would be a structure with three elements. At the core would be the executive arm of the mayor's office and the elected authority, facilitating the construction and agreement of a shared vision, setting up structures for implementation and being democratically accountable for delivering desired change in London. They would in a sense look up to a cross sector assembly for guidance and support as well as scrutiny. And they would look sideways to a raft of cross sectoral implementing agencies which would strike a balance between autonomy and accountability.

Finally, to ensure probity, in the aftermath of some malpractice in governance in the UK, we recommend the establishment of a London Audit Office to audit London's governance, created primarily by secondment from, and working with, the Audit Commission and the national Audit Office.

We now consider each of these three elements in more detail.

THE MAYOR AND THE GREATER LONDON AUTHORITY

The mayor would be elected London-wide. In line with our earlier analysis, people need to feel that they are an active part of the process and therefore a system of transferable votes is desirable to ensure that the mayor has an absolute majority in first and second preferences over all other candidates.

The members of the Greater London Authority would be elected on a constituency, not a London-wide basis. Given the growing importance of sub regions in London, the election of a number (see below) of members in each of five constituencies based on the five sub regions of North, South, East, West and Central would seem the most appropriate solution. The exact definition of boundaries, whilst no doubt contentious, is not insuperable. They need to be related to the functional roles of the sub regions.

Constituencies based on borough boundaries appears to be retrospective and could lead to pressure for members to be mandated by their political colleagues at borough level. Whilst this hardly existed in effect in the GLC, it was an historically different situation with the boroughs being created at the same time as the GLC. Now the boroughs have a tradition of over 30 years governance at the local level and have shared some strategic functions since the demise of the GLC. The fact that there would only be one member per constituency is also unhelpful for a variety of reasons expanded upon below.

Boundaries which were to follow those of the Euro constituencies make no particular sense in terms of London-wide governance, nor the governance of sub areas within it.

The sub-regional approach, therefore appears to be the most appropriate. Again, in line with our earlier analysis, a transparently fair system of election is essential and we believe that *proportional representation, or a close variant based upon it,* would be a logical solution. The election of only one representative per constituency would not allow this and seems unacceptable.

If the GLA is to be representative in the wider sense, which we believe is essential, there are real issues around equality at the electoral stage; thereafter key posts and responsibilities will be allocated from the fixed pool of those elected. We suggest the widest use of best possible practice (including positive action) to encourage candidates who represent all London in terms of race, gender and people with disabilities. The White Paper should contain specific proposals on this in order to ensure accountability.

The numbers of members per constituency is critical. The numbers need to be large enough to promote proportional representation, to provide real political debate and the attraction of a wide range of candidates to facilitate equality. On the other hand, the total number of members across London needs to be small enough to guarantee that most have a real role to play in the new structure (hence attracting serious and competent candidates). In terms of the equality of representation, the numbers of members per constituency will need to vary if there are significant differences in the numbers of registered electors in each constituency.

If the total membership of the Authority is to be restricted as suggested in the

Green Paper, then there would be an average of 4 or 5 members in each constituency. If the argument for greater representation is agreed, we believe that between 7 and 10 elected members from each of the 5 constituencies would be appropriate, giving an Authority of about 40 members.

The key relationship between the members and the mayor would lie in that between the mayor and a number of commissioners drawn from their number. The totality of the membership would be the pool of talent from which the commissioners would be selected. This concept of responsibility being held by a mayor and a 'cabinet' is, in line with our key principles, more inclusive and representative than a mayor acting alone. Before setting out the formal relationship between the mayor and the commissioners however we need to discuss the roles that the commissioners would carry out.

Commissioners would be of two kinds. First, those who in the broadest sense would commission work from the implementing agencies. The commissioners would work with the agencies to ensure that their draft strategies reflected the London Vision, be the conduit for money flowing from the mayor's office to the agency, and be the main point of contact between the agency and the authority and mayor. It would be an enabling function, facilitating the autonomy of the agency whilst maintaining links to political and democratic accountability.

Second, there would be commissioners for the four sub regions of the North, South, East and West. There could either be a fifth commissioner for central London, or the mayor could take this role. If the mayor were to act as the commissioner for the central area, it could be argued that this would give too much power to that sub region. In practice the opposite may be true. The mayor, under any system, will receive powerful lobbying from those with strong interests in central London. If the mayor were made formally the commissioner for central London, and given his/her overarching responsibility for London, s/he would have to temper any zeal s/he might have for central London in the wider interests of the capital and its other sub regions.

The role of the sub-regional commissioners would be to look across the work of the agencies from a sub-regional perspective, to make recommendations on the strategic priorities of their sub regions, to advocate budgetary allocations to enable the various implementing partnerships that operate on a spatial basis (including existing major partnerships), and to act as the point of contact with the authority and the mayor. The boundaries of the sub regions would overlap (see section 4) to facilitate understanding of the knock-on benefit that can flow from action in one sub region into another.

We believe that this ability for the authority, via the two kinds of commissioners, to look simultaneously at the vertical division of responsibility held by different agencies and the horizontal needs of sub regions spanning across the different competencies of the agencies, is another aspect of good governance.

The selection of commissioners. Given the important role of the commissioners and the concept of a cabinet, the method of their selection is critical. One option would be for the mayor to appoint the commissioners - the 'functional' commissioners selected from the whole membership of the authority, the sub-regional ones from the sub regions. This model, whilst facilitating in principle a cohesive cabinet, raises issues about the re-establishment of a democratic deficit. There is a contradiction between having elections based on a version of proportional representation when the cabinet could contain members of only one party. The model sits uneasily with notions of inclusivity, partnership and joint working.

The alternative model is to have the functional commissioners elected by the membership of the authority (with allocations relating to party strengths as is current practice in local government) and sub-regional commissioners selected by the elected members of the sub-regional constituencies.

Whilst there is a good deal more that could be said in detail about the relationship between the different elements of the structure and on functions, they are of a different order to the issues on which we have concentrated. We close this section with brief comments on competencies, on constructing the vision and on resources.

Competencies

We agree broadly with the list of competencies listed in the Green Paper, but argue strongly that it will not be possible to decide definitely on the correct set of competencies once and for all in the Act. This is not seen as a compromise but as a strength to deal with rapid change in an uncertain climate.

The concept of a formal review of competencies should be built into the White Paper/Bill/Act from the start. We suggest a formal review after two years.

We stress that the authority needs to have, or have access to, the competence to meet its competencies. If the authority is to be 'slim' it follows that provision will need to be made to access outside organisations for assistance, either through secondments or commissioning. We hope that universities would play a major role here - along the line of that played in many of our European partner countries.

Constructing the Vision

We have argued above that one of the key functions of the mayor and authority will be drafting a relevant *Vision for the Future of London*. The way this is done and its inclusiveness, relevance, flexibility and the commitment to thorough analysis, evaluation and review, are all essential.

The vision needs to be all embracing, it should span beyond the competencies that the authority itself has. In a sense the authority is the 'client' for the services and provisions that London needs. Hence the Vision should include references to the 'client' needs of London for health, education, training etc. Where appropriate the vision should set out the service standards that are needed in these areas in the interests of London. It would also need to set out resource requirements, and this is discussed below.

The vision should include a wide range of potential outcomes. First, it should be clear about what the GLA will do itself. Second, it should contain clear policies that are *binding* upon others (e.g. in the field of land use planning). Third, it should be clear about what it will seek to achieve through partnership and joint ventures. Finally, it should be clear about what it is exhorting others to do in the interests of London and set out how it will negotiate and enable these things to happen.

Resources

In many ways this is the most crucial issue of all, and the Green Paper is comparatively silent on it. One can see from the emphasis in the Green Paper, and absence of taxing powers, what might be in mind or what indeed might be the outcome. The mayor will be able to deploy planning powers (like the LDDC) to attract investors, offering leverage funding derived from central government. This could be the mayor's main activity, giving rise to transport and inward investment initiatives, but one has to ask whether it is enough.

An entirely different function of government is to ensure justice between citizens and competing interests, to bring democratic pressure to bear on private interests to ensure that public interests (where they conflict) and the interests of the weak are respected. Elected governments have a responsibility also to address issues of social exclusion in the interests of the individual and the common interest too. Neither of these can they do without some direct access to resources which are not beholden either to the private sector or a remoter tier of government. The concept of subsidiarity does not come to a halt at the boundary of resource allocation.

This is not to argue that the GLA needs a huge budget, nor even that an arrangement cannot be made which respects the commitment to no overall growth in expenditure. The starting point is to acknowledge that the need is real and, if not addressed, will undermine credibility of the mayor and the authority from the start.

This issue is the one on which the greatest clashes between central and city-wide government in London have concentrated in the past. To ignore or bury it does not mean that it will go away. Some, albeit limited, access to resources appears to be as crucial to the democratic mandate in London as they are to the Scottish Assembly. Even if the arguments for the balance of market power and the need to address social exclusion were ignored, there remains a case for the use of public resources as an essential tool for generating leverage. To enter the field of brokering partnerships to achieve a wider agenda in London's interests without the ability to bring some resources to the table is a hopeless task. Some method of allocating capital resources commensurate with the need for priority action must be found. Presumably, if there is to be no overall increase in resources, it will have to come from 'top slicing' existing capital programmes. Specific borrowing powers will also be needed, with the limits set as necessary by the Secretary of State.

On the revenue side, there are a number of possibilities which the White Paper might usefully float for further comment and development. One is for the GLA to have a power of general competence, similar to that given to local authorities, being able to raise 2 per cent of the local rate for such purposes. This would replace the borough's power (to achieve nil growth), but the GLA would have to define its need and be accountable for its proper and effective use. Another would be a visitor tax, as is now very common elsewhere. If it is felt that such issues should not be included in the White Paper, then the possibility of including the general issue in the referendum, on the Scottish model, could be further considered.

We see public money being allocated to the mayor's office, not to the authority or the assembly. There a variety of reasons for this, but the most important is for the mayor to have at his/her disposal the ability to take action and facilitate change. However the mayor would be accountable ultimately to the public electorally and, via the authority, for the proper and relevant use of the budget. They would have their budget debated by the assembly and agreed by the authority and be open to scrutiny by backbenchers, the assembly and ultimately by the London Audit Office. Such tiers would be designed to provide a basis for a reasonable balance of power.

THE GREATER LONDON ASSEMBLY

We envisage the creation of a Greater London Assembly which is made up of a mix of representatives (not mandated delegates) from each sector - public, private, voluntary, employee and employer representatives, higher and further education etc. Each sector would form an electoral college which would elect their representatives (say four each) in an open and democratic way. This would probably be best achieved through umbrella bodies which have a regional or sub-regional focus such as the CBI, LCCI, LVSC. Issues of representation from an equality perspective should be owned by the electoral colleges with the involvement of the mayor.

The purpose of the assembly would primarily be to provide wider involvement in the governance of London so that the commitment and expertise in the wider community can be brought to bear; it would provide public accountability as opposed to the democratic and executive accountability residing with the mayor.

The assembly would have statutory rights to:

- debate and approve the vision prepared by the mayor's office;
- debate the annual budget;
- comment on the strategic plans of the various agencies (see below);
- conduct transparent scrutiny hearings into budgetary spend and the achievement of outcomes;
- and, to ensure that the assembly was not purely reactive, it would conduct a major public debate, at the end of the first and third years of its four year term of office, into emerging issues and the need to review/ adjust the vision; it could call for reports from the mayor into critical emerging issues.

The assembly would elect its own chair; any individual could take the chair only once, for a period lasting two years.

THE IMPLEMENTING AGENCIES

The number, and to some extent, the nature of these will be affected by the competencies which ultimately reside with the Greater London Authority. An agency, for example as in the case of the London Development agency, may be needed for each main competency. The fact that new agencies may be set up, and others closed when their job is done or subsumed by a more relevant agency, is a strength which enables the structure as a whole to change over time - achieving flexibility within continuity.

Nonetheless there are certain organisational principles which we feel should affect all agencies, flowing again from the general principles which we have set out above.

First, all agencies should be cross-sectoral in order for the governance of London to benefit directly from a wide range or experience and expertise. The potential range of sectors is the same as the assembly, and the issue of representation from an equality perspective will again be critical.

The membership should be by election through electoral colleges, they should not be by direct appointment by the mayor as this would undermine ownership. The mayor should however have the right to nominate two additional members to any agency where this will demonstrably assist in the representational framework or to provide additional specialist expertise.

The Chair of the Boards of the agencies should be elected by the Board itself for a two year term.

The Board would receive some of its funding form the mayor's office via their relevant commissioner. It would prepare its strategy/corporate plan in the context of the London Vision and refer this, via the commissioner to the Authority for approval. Within that context it should have maximum autonomy to deliver, but be subjected to accountability via the commissioner.

The sub regions

We have argued above that sub regions are likely to play an increasingly important economic role in establishing the difference of 'place' in a globalised world. Few people, for example, would have difficulty in distinguishing the different functional roles of West London (with its specific activity centres of Heathrow, Park Royal and Wembley); Central London (with its historic, governmental, trading and financial core) and East London (with its rapidly improving infrastructure links with mainland Europe and large development sites). These sub regions are complemented by the industrial centres and opportunities of North London (reflected in the grant of Objective 2 status under the ERDF) and South London (where recent work has more clearly defined the coherence of the sub region).

We also argue that in the realm of social exclusion there are clear patterns which are better understood at the sub-regional level, as are the opportunities for creating the conditions for economic and social inclusion.

It will not be possible for a vision for London to offer a practical way forward unless it gets under the surface of what binds London together (important though that is) to look at difference (including the advantages that difference contains) and at complementarities between different parts of London. We believe that the locational, economic and social relevance of sub-regional strategies will form the bridge that links an overview of London's future to local delivery. They will not only link strategy and action, but become the means to release implementation initiatives that are not accessible at the London-wide or local (borough) level. Two brief examples make the point.

First, the resolution of social exclusion in East London is essential to the well-being of London as a whole - but cannot be achieved by London-wide action or agencies. Similarly, no one Borough, no matter how well intentioned or resourced, can deal with the issues. The underlying causes of social exclusion and the phenomenon of residential transience will permanently recreate exclusion in East London unless they are tackled on a wider scale. Indeed we argue that it is *only* by looking at these issues sub-regionally, combining the correct spatial focus with a cross-sectoral approach, can solutions be revealed which are otherwise invisible.

Second, there is the question of 'anchoring'. By anchoring we mean the ability to retain wealth creating potential in an area and then seek to expand it. Anchoring is often used as a term referring only to the need to anchor large companies - for example the need to anchor Ford's to Dagenham - but we see its relevance also to anchoring SME networks and clusters in the sub region and to retain the outputs of HE institutions (in terms of a pool of talent) in their area. The sheer scale of support services required for successful anchoring, including relevant training and supply chains, cannot be provided by any one local agency. Nor can the required 'on the ground relevance' of the support systems be handed down from regional bodies. It is only at the sub-regional level that the combination of relevant scale and ownership becomes possible. Mechanisms to ensure their delivery in London are currently absent, compared with the best examples of continental practice.

The list could be expanded, but the point is made. UEL is currently engaged in a research exercise looking in more detail at those functions, actions and services that can be more effectively provided at the sub-regional level than at any other. This work will feed into the London Study.

We have argued (earlier in this paper) that the economic and functional importance of sub regions is going to grow. This importance is also being fuelled by the insistence of the major funding regimes, in the EU and the UK, that significant funds will only go to programmes that can demonstrate, in effect, their sub-regional impact. In their train, these projects are creating a series of sub-regional partnerships/monitoring committees to implement and assess them. We see this tendency as increasing. The case for attracting Objective 2 status to London stemmed from the successful disaggregation of large areas of decline in North/East London from the overall position of wealth and strength of London as a whole. The specific problems, and opportunities, of sub regions in London will always be masked by the general affluence of the capital unless they are analysed at the correct level.

We have also argued that sub regions contain certain characteristics (viz. social exclusion) which need addressing, as well as certain opportunities and policy options that can only be realised at the sub-regional level. If this analysis is correct, two questions need to be addressed in the context of this paper; what are London's sub regions, and do they need a specific tier of government?

The two questions are in fact inter-related; one cannot be fully answered without reference to the other. However, it is easier to look at the question of government first.

In the abstract, the answer to the question as to whether a sub-regional tier of government is needed would hang on the number and range of those functions which are better organised at spatial levels less than Greater London but wider than borough level, and on the definition and relative autonomy of the sub regions themselves. In practice, the question is not really on the agenda. No one is seriously considering, nor are we proposing, an additional tier of government between the region (Greater London) and the boroughs.

If, for the foreseeable future, there is no practical case for sub-regional government, the question still arises as to whether there is a need for some form of sub-regional governance. Here we think that there is an over-riding case to be made in favour. If it is correct that different sub regions in London have clearly different structural characteristics (albeit over-lapping in some instances), if it is correct that some functions and actions are best carried out at that level, then it follows that some strategies, implementation packages and evaluation systems are required at that level - in the context of an overall Vision for London. Those strategies need to be based on an appropriate knowledge of the area and a real commitment to seeing them through. Hence our proposal for sub-regional commissioners (without the bureaucracy of another tier of government).

Such a concept would however be incomplete without reference to sub-regional partnerships - not least because it could be argued that a fusion of existing large partnerships could perform the role of governance in the sub regions. We argue that sub-regional partnerships and sub-regional governance are not the same thing. There are a number of excellent sub-regional partnerships that already exist; but they were not set up with governance in mind. They have an established role and 'turf'. Their role has often grown out of the need to bid for resources, or to bring together business interests in an area. Some of them are single issue partnerships covering a large area, some of them are multi-faceted covering smaller areas. They were not designed to, nor do they, form a coherent pattern across the capital, nor do they collectively cover the range of interests and activities that we would argue form the basis of an effective sub-regional focus.

They are, and should remain, a great force for implementation and hence asset in achieving the Vision for London.

There is also the question of a democratic deficit at the sub-regional level. The growth in partnerships has changed the climate from one where local authority leaders initially gained an expanding role in community governance to one which poses a real threat to local leadership. Partnerships have grown from one-to-one partnerships between a local authority and, say, a local firm, to more complex partnerships covering a significant part of a local area (viz. City Challenge) to partnerships which cover very large areas seeking to knit together a wide range of interests that no longer conform to local authority boundaries and over which, consequently, no one can claim legitimate democratic representation. This new geography is unfamiliar to local government; the information flows, institutions and structures are not in place to secure leadership and vision.

The way forward, we propose, is for the existing partnerships to be supported and built upon as significant agencies for the delivery of sub-regional strategies (which would be developed under the umbrella of the Greater London Authority's Vision for London). They would also have links to the various functional agencies (London Development Agency etc.) set up to implement the overall Vision, and to their sub-regional commissioner.

This leads into the second question - how many sub regions should there be, and what are the most appropriate boundaries?

It has been argued elsewhere (*Rising East* Volume1 Issue 1) that there are three clear functional sub regions within London - West, Central and East. We will not repeat the arguments here. Not surprisingly, there is some disquiet amongst institutions representing or active in South and North London about an analysis that concentrates on the West, Central and East. When the issue of sub regions as functional entities is put in the wider context of governance, and in the particular context of regional government and electoral constituencies, other considerations come into play. Taking these into account, we believe that a division of London into the five sub regions of North, South, West, Central and East is appropriate, pragmatic and likely to prove politically acceptable.

No amount of data analysis leads to the 'correct' definition of the number of sub regions (it will help however in defining their boundaries). A basic reason for this is that the boundary of Greater London itself has no particular logic and so an attempt to define parts of the area in this way is doomed to failure. The exercise would inevitably also contain a large number of value judgements with which not all would agree. There are other concerns which we refer to below in a discussion about the definition of boundaries. In short, a pragmatic judgement is needed, and it seems to us that our five suggested sub regions link a view of functional distinctiveness with an appropriate basis for electoral constituencies as argued above.

Turning to the question of boundaries, it is clear that there are some difficult issues to be addressed. For some purposes, particularly electoral purposes, an absolute definition is needed - people must be clear in which constituency they can vote. But for most other purposes boundaries tend either to create dispute and/or create arbitrary division where continuity is preferable.

In any event, we argue that in reality it is impossible to define exact boundaries on a multi-functional basis for sub regions in London. For example, a boundary that may be ideal for health-care purposes would almost certainly be inappropriate for waste collection, and bear no relation to travel to work zones. There is no point in pretending that a 'rational' solution exists.

In the spirit of the innovative approach to governance that we advocate at the start of this paper, we propose that, whereas the constituencies should have a definite boundary, the sub regions should not. Borrowing from the concept of 'fuzzy logic', we propose overlapping boundaries for the sub regions, with the express purpose of encouraging the development of notions of complementarity rather than competition between areas.

The University of East London is currently looking at data that might prove helpful in defining the five constituency boundaries.

Research and information

Research, information and analysis will be critical to the relationships between the component parts of London's governance and to relationships with London's residents and interests generally.[2]

THE LONDON RESEARCH AND INFORMATION AGENCY

We assume that the authority will have its own core policy staff. Beyond this, we propose the creation of a statutorily-independent London Research and Information agency (LRIA). This would serve the information needs of the authority, assembly and agencies. It should have a management board composed of nominees from the authority, from London's agencies, the London boroughs and from representing other key information and research bodies, e.g. universities. It will provide the mayor with key data and analysis for policy formulation, review etc. and for scrutiny of the practical relevance of outcomes.

Information generated by the LRIA should be in the public domain. The principal task of the LRIA should be to ensure that the public political process of governing London is able to be as informed as possible about

London's condition and needs. We envisage that the LRIA would not carry out all the research itself, nor have the wide-ranging competencies to do so. It should carry out clear tendering processes for all work that is to be put out.

DEMOCRACY HOUSE

It should be possible for any Londoner, any London politician, any tax payer, any journalist, analyst or researcher to obtain information about the expenditure of public monies, except in the limited and defined circumstances where personal or commercial confidentiality is legitimate.

A key part of this access to information, as regards the public sector, is being able to know what decisions have been taken and by whom. We propose, akin to the model of Companies House, the creation of 'Democracy House' - a physical and on-line resource which would have the statutory duty of housing all minutes and annual reports of Greater London's authority, agencies, assembly, and boroughs. It would also house the annual reports of all organisations in London funded by any part of London's governance which would be obliged to detail the public funds they had received and to account for their appropriate expenditure.

Conclusions

There should be the visible and effective presence in London's government of sufficient 'representative capacity' for it truly to be able to reflect and work for all London. Its claim to be able to facilitate desirable change will rest in its representative capacity at least as much as in its competence.

It has to be able to work on a multi-level political playing field and to have reasonable freedom to do so. It should not only have the 'right of subsidiarity' from UK government, but recognise the importance of local democracy at borough level. In turn, UK Government has to support local government's new alignment with regional government. The GLA is rightly not set up to be a multi-purpose service authority along the lines of the GLC. The capability of borough councils should be supported rather than the GLA increasingly encroach on what should be local discretion simply because the depredations of the post-1979 period have not been repaired.

The ability to deal with or adjust to change is essential. It should be recognised that while the 'democratic core' must be maintained, the administrative and organisational arrangements which are the expressions of its power and decisions will have to evolve. The GLA should have sufficient competence to make such changes itself, perhaps through recourse to London referenda, without requiring an Act of Parliament for every alteration.

We conclude by repeating our belief that the creation of London governance needs to flow from a coherent set of principles that are relevant to their time. Only in this way can the proposals be internally consistent and have an above average chance of appropriateness, acceptability and survival.

We believe that the principles that we have set out in this paper and the implications that flow from them meet this requirement.

We started by stressing that there was a real opportunity in London to devise at this time an exemplary model of regional governance. We believe that old structures are no longer relevant, but in making changes, democratic representation and powers need to be defended and redefined. A directly elected mayor, and an authority elected by some form of proportional representation and having some tax raising powers, elected through sub-regional constituencies and electing sub-regional commissioners could revitalise the conventional political process. The formation of the cross sectoral assembly and implementing agencies could give access to a more pluralist polity without over-riding the proper lines of democratic authority.

Within this framework there are clear choices, particularly around issues to do with the numbers of members of the authority; with the relationship between the mayor and the commissioners and how the former are elected or appointed; with the balance of responsibility held by the mayor, commissioners, authority and assembly; and with tax raising powers.

However those choices are resolved, the critical issue is to ensure exemplary and sustainable good governance in this great World City as we enter the new Millennium.

This submission has been prepared by Professor Drew Stevenson for the University of East London's East London Group which works on regeneration and governance issues. The paper does not therefore represent the corporate view of the University of East London.

NOTES

1. This article was originally submitted in response to the Secretary of State's consultative Green Paper on the Governance of London.

2. An appendix sets out short responses to the specific questions raised in the Green Paper - but the fuller responses, and some wider issues that cannot be dealt with by limiting a response to the issues raised in the questions themselves, are covered in the body of the paper. A second appendix refers to the role of the university in making this response. Copies of both appendices are available from The Docklands and East London Regeneration Unit, University of East London, Duncan House, High Street, Stratford, London E15 2JB.

A very social capital:

Measuring the vital signs of community life in Newham

Greg Smith

Analysis of organisations in the voluntary and community sector in the London Borough of Newham indicates what at first glance appears as a vibrant, diverse and growing network of community organisations. However *Greg Smith* argues that the evidence suggests a more pessimistic interpretation. The existence of a large and active state funded voluntary sector is no guarantee of a thriving civil society or high levels of social capital in the population at large.

The concept of social capital

The concept of social capital is a useful metaphor which suggests that a society with a rich web of relationships and widespread participation in community organisations will flourish, and that individuals who hold large accumulations of social capital will be at an advantage over others with less.[1] Early definitions of the concept go back as far as Hanifan (1920) who was very involved in the community centre movement of the time:

> In the use of the phrase 'social capital'... We do not refer to real estate or to personal property or to cash, but rather to that in life which tends to make those tangible substances count for most in the daily lives of people: namely good will, fellowship, sympathy, and social intercourse among the individuals and families who make up a social unit. ... If a person comes into contact with his neighbours, there will be an accumulation of social capital, which may immediately satisfy his social needs and which may bear a social potentiality sufficient for the substantial improvement of life in the whole community.

... First, then, there must be an accumulation of community social capital. (which may be) effected by means of public entertainments, picnics, and a variety of other community gatherings.(pp78-9)

The term social capital was used by Jane Jacobs in *The Death and Life of Great American Cities* in 1961 in reference to networks in urban neighbourhoods: 'These networks are a city's irreplaceable social capital. Whenever the capital is lost, from whatever cause, the income from it disappears, never to return until and unless new capital is slowly and chancily accumulated'.

A more theoretical sociological interest in the concept was developed by Bourdieu (1972) who states that 'social capital is the sum of the resources, actual or virtual, that accrue to an individual or a group by virtue of possessing a durable network of more or less institutionalized relationships of mutual acquaintance and recognition'. The theory of social capital is worked out most fully by Coleman (1990) which has become one of the most cited key references in the contemporary literature in the field.

Wellman and colleagues in Canada have used the concept of social capital in the study of personal support networks employing the techniques of social network analysis to good effect in its measurement. (Wellman 1979, Wellman and Wellman 1992, Wellman and Wortley 1990). Friedland and McLeod (forthcoming) have applied the theory to the mass media and highlighted the role of the local press in community integration. The project for the reconstruction of civil society in Eastern Europe and the former Soviet Union has generated much discussion of the theory of social capital (e.g. Kolankiewicz and the rejoinder by Pahl 1996, Mai 1997). Some have argued that a similar civil society project is needed in western countries such as the UK. (Knight and Stokes 1996).

Recent debates on the concept of social capital have been triggered and envigorated by the work of Putnam and Fukuyama. Putnam's study of community organisations in Italy (1993) suggest that regions with a strong and lively range of voluntary activity are likely to develop more rapidly economically than regions where social capital is lower. The role of 'trust' in this process is highlighted and developed further in Fukuyama (1995). A whole issue of *American Behavioral Scientist* has been devoted to the debate on social capital covering the link with religion (Greeley 1997), community organising (Wood 1997), democracy (Newton 1997), social theory (Foley and Edwards 1997), social movements (Minkoff 1997), civic engagement (Heying 1997, Kenworthy 1997) and minority communities (Portney and Berry 1997).

More recently Putnam (1995a, 1995b) has argued that social capital and trust has been declining in American society since about 1945, resulting in a society where many individuals go 'bowling alone'. Much of the decline he believes can be attributed to the influence of television, although this is contested by Norris (1996). One might also consider the privatising and delocalising influence of the personal automobile in the same time period.

Concern about loss of community is echoed among communitarian political thinkers such as Etzioni (1994) who advances the proposition that the contemporary western world is besotted with the notion of individual rights and in consequence suffers from a deficit, in parenting skills as well as in the vitality of civil society. Such thinking has permeated the outlook and policy of British governments even before the New Labour victory at the 1997 election. This has resulted in a rhetoric (and sometimes an improved practice) majoring on partnership approaches and stakeholder involvement in such fields as urban regeneration and health and social welfare services (Smith 1996, Burkett and Ashton 1996). Popular participation, and community development do appear to have a more important place in urban policy than at any time in the last two decades. Developing and accumulating social capital is thus clearly on the policy agenda for urban regeneration, and could have great importance in the future development of the East London region. A recent Rowntree funded study of urban regeneration partnerships investigates how networks emerge and operate in this context and suggests sustained regeneration and new forms of community governance depend on how these networks are supported and maintained over future years (Skelcher *et al* 1996).

Wilson (1997) has set out a comprehensive agenda for building social capital in economic development, while Mitlin and Thomson (1995) present and discuss case studies of participation including the British 'planning for real' projects. Schusterman and Hardoy (1997) review the long-term process of reconstructing social capital in a poor *barrio* in Buenos Aires and argue that long-term resources and commitment which can be flexibly applied as conditions change are a pre-requisite for sustainable development. They critique the usual approach of 'projects' evaluated by 'quantified outcomes' measured over a couple of years.

If urban policy is increasingly to be based on the case that the accumulation of social capital brings economic prosperity, the mechanisms linking social capital to economic growth are worthy of detailed investigation. A strong version of the Putnam/Fukuyama hypothesis would posit that a high level of social capital is a necessary or sufficient prior cause of strong economic life. A weaker version would be content to say that the two are merely correlated. One could perhaps argue the reverse, that a strong economy is a necessary basis for the growth of social capital in a community although this position appears counter intuitive. A more well established (if rather romanticised) view is that community solidarity and mutual help arises as a response to shared poverty and oppression. In this account social capital is developed as compensation for lack of economic capital. However, it must be pointed out that at the same time as slum dwellers were forming strong communities capitalist elites were also building up networks of power and solidarity on the basis of the proverbial 'old school tie'.

Recent green economic theory following Schumacher's *Small is Beautiful* (1973) suggests a curvilinear relationship with the economy as the controlling variable. A briefing paper from Friends of the Earth and the (Whitechapel-based) New Economics Foundation for the 1997 Election (FOE/NEF 1997) suggests 'the presence of stable social capital is a prerequisite for market growth, but after the threshold point (where growth ceases to be beneficial because of long term environmental and human costs), the destruction of social capital by markets contributes to the insecurity and decline of society'.

Before applying the notion of social capital in the local context it is worth pausing to review and question the implicit values and ideological basis of the theory. From a certain perspective the debate about social capital can appear progressive, it does after all appear to represent a more humane and holistic understanding of society than the economic determinism of Marxism or the brutal free market individualism of the New Right. However, it is, to say the least, a pity that the language of the market and of money has been co-opted, or perhaps more accurately has colonised, discourse about the relationships between human beings, which traditionally have been seen as outside the cash economy. There is a danger that the notion of social capital will come to be taken as something more than a useful metaphor, and that qualities which on any humanistic or spiritual values should be rated as 'more precious than rubies, yea than much fine gold' could be reduced to balances on accountants' spreadsheets. This creeping commodification of qualities such as gift exchange, voluntary labour, solidarity, mutuality, neighbourliness and friendship is to be regretted and resisted. Certainly the Christian tradition of social involvement as expressed in Catholic social teaching, documents such as the recent Catholic bishops' document on *The Common Good* (CBC 1996) , and the 1985 *Faith in the City* report (ACUPA 1985) all make an assumption that community, in the form of localised *gemeinschaft* is a moral imperative and a good in its own right. While Putnam may (or may not) be empirically correct in suggesting that high levels of social capital lead to economic prosperity, one cannot help being reminded of the words of Jesus that we 'should seek first the Kingdom of God and all these things shall be added unto you'.

Social capital and 'the East End community spirit'

The folk history of the East End, coloured as it usually is by the rose-tinted spectacles of socialism, suggests that in the past East London made up for its lack of economic capital by large accumulations of social capital. (The same suggestion is made for Hamburg in the 1990s by Dangshat 1994). East London was a community of working-class people who were exploited by capital and therefore never had any control of the means of production or the capital accumulated from it. In so far as social capital developed it was the survival solidarity of an oppressed people. East London has been portrayed as the birthplace of organised Labour with the strikes of the dockers and match girls in the late nineteenth century as high water marks of working-class solidarity. Certainly West Ham elected Keir Hardie as the first Independent Labour Party MP while the Poplarism of George Lansbury in the 1920s represents some evidence of popular involvement in municipal socialism. Marriott's (1991) study highlights the importance of the Co-operative retailing movement. But despite the political hegemony of the Labour Party and the strength of the trade unions, local working people never got their hands on the economic levers. Even the post-war nationalisation of transport and the docks failed to protect the East End against the effects of the global transformations of capitalism of the final quarter of the century.

Thus social capital in East London had little by way of economic infrastructure. It was reduced rather to two ideas: community spirit and provision of municipal services, most notably housing. The settlements, missions and churches also played an important part in social welfare and community building, even through such low key activities as charabanc trips to Southend (Marchant 1986). The Blitz engendered a spirit often remembered as community singing in the bomb shelters. In early post war years the Bethnal Green community studies of Young and Wilmott (1957) perpetuated the stereotype, of cheerful Cockney neighbourhoods, knit together by local kinship obligations and a general sociability of the streets. (Interestingly Coleman 1990, mentions the Bethnal Green study as an example of a community where mutual obligations, helpfulness and trust are evidence of high social capital.) Slum clearance, tower block estates, the exodus from the inner city to Dagenham and beyond, and the influx of immigrants are often blamed for the breakdown of community spirit. 'It's no longer safe to go out at nights, let alone leave your door open or your key under the mat' is a refrain that is often heard from older white East Enders and which is frequently reinforced by the media. However, it could be argued that a key causal factor in the alleged decline of social capital has been the economic collapse of the area. People with little or no economic stake in society, with no jobs to go to, and therefore with reduced social contact with others, living in under-resourced and rapidly changing neighbourhoods, with tensions which breed conflict and crime, are perhaps even more likely than the successful entrepreneur to retreat into a privatised existence, where 'me first' appears as the best survival strategy.

East London is widely recognised as one of the largest and most persistent concentrations of economic decline, urban deprivation and associated social problems, and despite massive regeneration in Docklands is struggling to develop a more positive image which will attract investment. The borough of Newham, in which the research reported here took place, is ranked by the Department of Environment's index of local conditions based on the 1991 Census (DoE 1994) as the most deprived local authority district in England. It is also the most ethnically diverse (in 1991 42 per cent were from ethnic minorities). In consequence community activity takes place in a context of lack of and declining resources, widespread poverty, and statutory services which are hard pressed to meet extremely high levels of need. Yet personal involvement in local life over many years leads me to the impression that 'there is a lot going on'. Need combined with diversity of the population has led to a wide range of community and voluntary sector activity, from charities for children and the aged which go back centuries, to refugee support groups and immigration rights campaigns that are being formed today.

However, a more sceptical working hypothesis has been adopted in most of our recent studies carried out at Aston Community Involvement Unit (CIU). The proposition is that public participation in organised social, political and community life in Newham does not amount to much, and is in all probability declining. The seeming vitality of the voluntary sector may in fact mask the reality. Voluntary organisations proliferate, especially in a context where funding, contracting out of services, and political influence are mediated through increasingly bureaucratic procedures. The experience of the CIU is that new groups by the score draw up constitutions and apply for charitable status. However the democratic accountability of such groups exists largely only on paper, few of them have large membership bases, and usually have difficulty finding a full complement of trustees. Indeed contested elections at AGMs appear rare and many meetings struggle to become quorate. One suspects that a small elite of professional voluntary sector employees, many of whom do not even live in the borough have accumulated the lion's share of social capital, (and project income in the form of salaries). As the public resources available to the local community are inadequate and declining, the funding that does get allocated may even represent a diversion from community activism towards the voluntary or rather 'not for profit' management of state resources for welfare service delivery. The rhetoric of community capacity building probably has little impact in terms of the accumulation of social capital by local residents. Nor incidentally does it seem to encourage shared ownership of public resources, such as public buildings or a co-operative approach to economic development.

In order to test this hypothesis it would be necessary to carry out a range of more detailed studies of a large representative sample of Newham residents alongside work on the voluntary sector organisations, and the regeneration partnerships and programmes in the area. Although it has been beyond our resources to do this in a systematic way, a number of small studies and secondary data from larger pieces of research produce some evidence which bears on this issue.

Measuring social capital

It is not easy to evaluate claims for historical change in the levels of social capital in East London. Memory is notoriously unreliable as a guide and there are few, if any, time series data sets which allow for relevant and consistent longitudinal measurement of this variable. The pluralism of the area, its ethnic diversity and the impact of globalisation on economy, culture and communications make the task more difficult still. However, for a baseline study it should be possible to address the issue by collating data on the following variables. Many of them, and variants on them have been used elsewhere by other researchers on this theme (e.g. Putnam 1995, Knight and Stokes 1994, Marshall 1995, Reynolds, Elsdon and Stewart 1995, Knight 1993):

a) Number of voluntary and community sector organisations. Their characteristics and role;

b) their network connectivity to other organisations both inside and outside the sector;

c) levels of membership in these organisations;

d) public awareness these organisations and use of the service they provide;

e) active citizen participation in religious, voluntary and community organisations;
f) formal citizen participation in local politics, and local elections;
g) informal personal localised networks including kin, neighbour and friendship relationships;
h) participation in families and multi-person households.

There is no intention here to suggest that these variables can all or indeed should be measured on reliable quantifiable scales. Still less is there any attempt to combine them into a single index, or unit of currency in which social capital can be counted, banked or exchanged. To use a European analogy, there is little prospect of an easy transition to monetary union, there may not even be a single market in terms of social capital. For example, Xavier de Souza Briggs (see note 1) when talking of the social capital resources available to individuals distinguishes between *support capital,* 'which helps people cope with problems posed by their circumstances ('get by'), this type is very often provided by socially similar others' and *leverage capital* 'which helps people change their life chances or create and take advantage of opportunities ('get ahead'), this type calls for having diverse ties, whether weak or strong'.

Our list of factors to examine betrays the fact that in this paper the focus will be on what Coleman (1990) has called the 'public good facet' of social capital rather than 'the private good facet ... how my connections can help me...'. However, it is obvious that there are likely to be large variations in levels of social capital between individuals and in all probability interesting correlations with key demographic variables, such as age, gender, social class and ethnicity.

The data presented below can only give partial coverage of the variables outlined above and bear on the general hypothesis that social capital in Newham is only thinly distributed, or monopolised by elites. We have, for example, little reliable data to hand on the membership levels or participation rates in community organisations (other than the churches), and nothing systematic on the role of professional workers in the local voluntary sector. However, we can present some findings which use social network analysis, based on relational data. The methods of social network analysis (Scott 1992, Freeman *et al* 1989, Wellman and Wortley 1992) seem particularly apposite to the measurement of social capital, and are being looked at with renewed interest by researchers in community and voluntary sector studies, although published results of empirical studies in the UK are as yet hard to come by.

Mapping the voluntary and community sector

HOW MANY ORGANISATIONS?

Newham has a large, lively but diverse and uncoordinated range of community and voluntary sector activity. It is also increasingly well documented and information about it is becoming more widely and easily accessible thanks to new electronic technologies. Recent research work by the Aston Community Involvement unit includes the development and updating of a directory/ database of religious groups and a survey of provision for young people (funded through the Newham Safer Cities Project). Information from this research has been incorporated into the LBN Social Services *Community Care Database*. Version 2.6 showed that in 1997 there were 790 groups or organisations classified as Newham voluntary groups.[2] Another 257 'London Voluntary' and 265 'national voluntary' organisations are listed as offering services to the people of the borough. In addition the list gives 9 after school clubs, 51 assorted youth projects or organisations, 51 housing association projects, and 97 places of worship.

The structure of the LBN database does not make it easy to cross-tabulate or breakdown the numbers of groups into mutually exclusive sub categories. However it appears that some 223 listed organisations are religious of which 150 are in the Christian tradition, and just under a hundred are places of worship which broadly tallies with the evidence of Aston CIU's Directory of Religious Groups in Newham (2nd edition 1995). Around 230 groups have a prime focus or dominant membership drawn from the ethnic minority communities. 70 focus their work on people with illness or disability and 77 on the elderly (over 50s population). Over 350 examples of provisions for young people aged 9-25 were documented by the Safer Cities Survey and a further 160 possibly existing groups failed to respond to the survey (Crisp and Smith 1997). Over two thirds of the provisions for young people were located in the voluntary or community sector, albeit in several cases drawing on funding provided by the state.

However we interpret these figures it is clear that there is a lot of voluntary and community sector activity to be found in Newham. Roughly 1000 local organisations are available to serve and mobilise a population of some 215,000, approximately one organisation for every 215 people. Barry Knight (1993) found rather lower ratios of organisations to population in the two London boroughs he studied (1:361 in Inner London and 1:420 in Outer London). The Newham figure which is not precisely comparable because of possible differences in method, compares roughly with his figures for small towns in Wales and the West Country and is somewhat lower than the ratio in his Northern borough.

THE STRUCTURE OF THE VOLUNTARY SECTOR

It is impossible to understand and navigate through this mass of information if it remains no more than a long list of organisations, ordered within a crude taxonomy of simple categories or multiple keywords. To appreciate more fully the nature and structure of the community/voluntary sector, and what it represents in terms of social capital, it is helpful to have a mental map of the relationships within it, the patterns of collaboration and information sharing, referral practices between agencies, and the way they build alliances through affiliations to umbrella bodies. Another part of the picture is linkages between the voluntary sector and the Borough Council. It is perhaps significant that at least four prominent Newham councillors are staff members in major local voluntary organisations, and many others are active in or serve on the management committees of community groups.

A small pilot study carried out in 1995-96 by Aston CIU attempted to delineate some of the structural linkages between organisations.[3] The network questions focused on three areas, awareness of other groups in particular fields of work, referrals to other agencies and membership and participation in umbrella groups. The 41 respondents named between 4 and 39 agencies of which they were aware (mean 16.95) - Table 1 gives the categorisations. In response to the question 'which organisations do you regularly refer people on to and for what? (list up to six)' all except 7 of the 41 respondents mentioned

Table 1: Awareness of other agencies working in various fields

Type of agency	number mentioned
Welfare rights advice	29
Support for people with a particular illness or disability	47
Drug and alcohol misuse	18
Crime prevention initiatives	20
Safety of people on the streets	16
The needs of young people	39
The needs of older people	44
The needs of refugees	37
Domestic violence	20

at least one agency to who they referred, 4 mentioned 6, and 2 mentioned 8, making 125 links in all (average 3.0). In terms of umbrella organisations, coalitions and forums the 41 local agencies reported memberships in 78 wider bodies, of which 48 were local to the borough.[4]

Public participation: various measures

The analysis of the organisations in Newham's voluntary and community sector presented above does suggest that the quantity and structure of community activity should amount to a considerable total of social capital, in whatever units such a commodity might be measured. However, it is still reasonable to ask how big an impact all these organisations make upon the people of Newham. Is the general public aware of their existence, of the nature of the services they offer? How many people are formal members of such groups, and how many are active participants?

AWARENESS OF VOLUNTARY SECTOR SURVEY

The first piece of evidence comes from a small survey carried out in the autumn of 1995 by a group of medical students on placement at CIU. They interviewed a quota sample of some 116 Newham residents contacted in the street, mainly in Stratford. They asked respondents whether they had heard of or used the services of 24 actual and one fictional local voluntary sector organisations. Table 2 gives their findings. Levels of awareness of the organisations appeared very low; only 5 organisations, all with a significant national profile, plus the generic 'church /religious group' were recognised by a majority of respondents. And only the Citizens Advice Bureau and Church/religious scored higher than 10 per cent in terms of actual usage. Even allowing for the fact that this survey was carried out by 'amateurs' and cannot claim to be fully representative, it presents strong evidence that the profile of many of the voluntary sector groups is not very high. There is no evidence in this survey that the general public accumulates much social capital through participation in such groups.

PARISH SURVEY; QUESTIONS ON LOCAL PARTICIPATION

Some corroboration of these findings comes from a church community survey carried out in 1992 by CIU with a local Anglican parish in Stratford/West Ham (Smith 1992). One hundred and eighty five residents were interviewed

Table 2: Public awareness of selected voluntary organisations

	not heard of	heard of	can contact	used
Neighbourhood Watch	11.2	69.8	13.8	5.2
Barnardos	23.3	60.3	14.7	1.7
Age Concern	29.3	55.2	15.5	0.0
Citizens Advice Bureau	10.3	49.1	28.4	12.1
Victim Support	41.4	49.1	7.8	1.7
Newham Council for Racial Equality	56.0	38.8	4.3	0.9
Newham Mind	56.9	37.9	3.4	1.7
Local Churches, mosques, temples	40.5	37.1	11.2	11.2
Tenants's Associations	60.3	33.6	6.0	0.0
Newham Rights	64.7	29.3	4.3	1.7
Advice Arcade	69.0	27.6	2.6	0.9
Refugee Centre	71.6	25.9	1.7	0.9
Newham Monitoring Project	75.0	21.6	3.4	0.0
Newham Parents Centre	73.3	19.8	3.4	3.4
Safezone Stratford	81.0	17.2	0.9	0.9
Community Links	80.2	17.2	1.7	0.9
Durning Hall	75.9	16.4	6.0	1.7
Councillor's surgery	81.0	16.4	1.7	0.9
Crossroads Care	85.3	14.7	0.0	0.0
Carers Association	82.8	13.8	1.7	1.7
Onelove Community Association	87.1	12.1	0.0	0.9
Upton Centre	90.5	6.9	1.7	0.9
N'ham Community Renewal Prog.	94.0	6.0	0.0	0.0
The Maister Smith Foundation **	96.6	3.4	0.0	0.0

**A fictitious organisation

on doorsteps selected by a random cluster sampling method. In response to the question. 'Which clubs, community groups and organisations are you a member of?'

One hundred and forty six (79 per cent) either said they belonged to none or gave no answer to this question. The remaining 39 mentioned 45 memberships; to a slightly different question 'do you or family go to a local community centre?' 26 people (14 per cent) said yes.

Respondents were also asked whether they participated in or attended a variety of different leisure activities. Apart from shopping and visiting relatives all these appeared to be minority pursuits. Furthermore the more participatory activities in which social capital might accumulate such as social clubs, pubs, adult education, religious groups and sports clubs attracted 30 per cent or less of the respondents. Even accounting for the possibility that the most clubbable people were under-represented in that they were more likely to be out when the interviewers knocked on their door these participation rates seem very low.

The data for children's participation is a little more encouraging. Of the 65 respondents with children only 2 reported that their offspring had not participated in any play scheme, children's or youth club, sports or uniformed organisation, although no single category attracted more than 30 per cent of the respondents' families.

SAFER CITIES PROJECT: SURVEY OF YOUTH PROVISION

A major piece of research carried out in late 1996 by CIU for the Newham Safer Cities Project (Crisp and Smith 1997) documented about 350 examples of provision for young people, the large majority of them (over two thirds) provided within and by the voluntary and community sector. The research defined 'young people' as those in the age range 9 to 25. The borough's population in this age range is estimated to be a little over 50,000 (one of the highest proportions in any district in the UK). A calculation based on questions to providing agencies about monthly usage of their services suggests Newham's provisions are used by an estimated 39,000 young people. At least 13,000 (and as many as 26,000 if multiple usage of services by individuals is taken into account) of the borough's 9-25 year olds are not accessing provision at all. From the point of view of the Safer Cities Project and society in general the argument that improved services for youth would reduce crime and the fear of crime has much to recommend it. It is at least plausible that young people who accumulate social capital, as well as the human and cultural capital that come through education, and some economic capital or at least income through employment, (in other words those who have a significant stake in the community), are less likely to have motives, opportunities and needs to commit crimes.

RELIGIOUS PARTICIPATION: THE 1994 DIRECTORY OF RELIGIOUS GROUPS

One sector of community life in which public participation is surprisingly high in Newham is religion. The 1994 Directory of Religious Groups documented 198 congregations and a further 77 'para-church' organisations operating within the borough (Aston CIU 1994, Smith 1996). Many of these churches and organisations were newly established and growing, others in a phase of renewal. There is also evidence of strong and active collaborative networking across the whole religious sector in Newham (Smith 1997). At the very least there appears in East London to be a 'blip' in the long-term process of secularisation and numerical church decline. It was estimated that some 18,000 people attended the Christian churches each week (8 per cent of the population or 11 per cent of the non-Asian population. The same research estimates that Newham has a Muslim community of up to 30,000 people, a Hindu community of some 21,000 and a Sikh community of over 4,000. A survey by the Newham Association of Faiths (reported in Smith 1996 and, in more detail, in Smith forthcoming) found weekly attendance at mosque by Muslim men as high as 75 per cent.

It must be admitted that participation in religious worship is a notoriously slippery variable to measure, as a result of its varying significance in different religious cultures, combined with the general problem of mismatch between survey findings based on reported attendance and harder data based on census counts in churches and mosques. It is nonetheless clear that the religious sector in Newham is full of vitality. While participation rates vary according to ethnicity, gender and social class, and religion is obviously an important factor in the construction of ethnic identity and belonging, meeting together on a regular basis in a religious community setting offers many individuals a rich opportunity for accumulating social capital. This is valuable to them first of all in terms of personal support networks, which help meet emotional, social and sometimes economic needs. Furthermore religious organisations can also provide a base for interventions in community development as evidenced by the large number of social welfare projects which have a religious foundation, and in mobilising in community politics. A significant example of this in recent years has been the formation of TELCO a broad based community organisation on the style of Saul Alinsky (Alinsky 1972, Farnell *et al* 1994) which has brought some 30 organisations into a coalition for political action, and seen mass meetings of up to 1500 people. Most of the member organisations are religious congregations with all of the major faith communities of East London represented.

POLITICAL PARTICIPATION

When we turn to local politics it seems that levels of active involvement in the parties is extremely low. Newham has the, not undeserved, reputation of being a one-party state, a place where Labour votes are weighed rather than counted. The only perceived threat to Labour at the present time comes, especially in the Docklands area, from the neo-Nazi British National Party and potentially in the North of the borough from Islamic mobilisation either inside or outside the party.

There is much evidence that the general public in Newham is not interested in politics. (In the West Ham parish survey only 8 per cent of respondents said they found politics to be very important, 25 per cent important and 66 per cent not important. In comparison the items rated very important were religion by 36 per cent of respondents, good health (89 per cent) family/home (89 per cent), work/education (59 per cent), a good standard of living (66 per cent) and taking part in the local community (23 per cent). Election turnout rates are an obvious variable that can be measured. At general elections Newham constituencies consistently report rates which are well below the national average figures, and below those for nearby constituencies, for example the marginal Ilford North and the safe Conservative Wanstead and Woodford. See Table 3. However, they are considerably higher than the record low 49 per cent national turnout reported for the US presidential election of 1996. Furthermore these percentages are based on an electoral roll which is liable to be more inaccurate and incomplete than those in other districts which do not have the same levels of population mobility, ethnic minorities and social exclusion. This means that any turnout figure would probably represent a smaller proportion of the adult population in Newham than in more settled, affluent and monochrome districts.

In council elections turnout is regularly much lower still. For example,

Table 3: General Election turnout - per cent of electorate

	1983	1987	1992	1994*	1997
Newham N.E.	62.1	64.1	60.3	(34.80)	
East Ham					60.3
Newham N.W	56.1	59.4	56.0		
West Ham					58.4
Newham South	53.6	59.1	60.2		
Poplar and Canning Town					58.5
Ilford North	71.3	72.6	77.9		71.6
Wanstead and Woodford Chingford &	68.4	72.4	78.2		
Woodford Green					70.7
UK National Average	72.7	74.3	77.7		71.3

Source: Elections archive web site QMW College[5]
* Parliamentary by-election

A very social capital

in the 1994 borough council elections turnout averaged 37 per cent only exceeding 40 per cent in five of the wards, all of which had a full range of candidates and were in some sense 'marginal'. Several wards in the old West Ham borough had turnout rates of 35 per cent or below and in one ward where only the Conservative party put up alternative candidates to Labour the turnout was less than 22 per cent.[6]

Labour Party membership may be a better measure of active political participation. Although it has almost doubled since the rebranded image of New Labour hit the supermarket shelves, membership of West Ham constituency stood, in September 1997, at 850 (600 of whom are fully paid up), rather than thousands. Active participation in branch meetings is even lower; Plashet ward, for example, has a reputation as a thriving and lively branch and has the largest membership of around 150. Two thirds of the members are male. However, monthly meetings are still usually less than a dozen people, coming from an increasingly wide range of ethnic and social class backgrounds. Obviously such low levels of participation make local branches very vulnerable to infiltration and takeover by any determined and well organised faction. Political structures in Newham make it easy for individuals and small groups to accumulate power and influence but they are hardly a rich bank of social capital for the community as a whole.

PERSONAL SUPPORT NETWORKS

Another area in which social capital can be accumulated and is susceptible of measurement is in the informal sector, the everyday relationships of social support. At the local level these are usually found in the links of kinship, friendship and neighbouring and numerous pieces of research in the tradition of community studies have investigated this area, for example, (Wilmott 1986,1987, Abrams/Bulmer 1986 Wellman 1979). In Newham the research evidence is limited and comes from the West Ham parish study (Smith 1992) and a follow up piece of work on neighbourhood networks carried out by a group of medical students on placement in 1993 (Smith 1994).

In the parish survey 185 respondents were asked 'how well do you know next door neighbours?' Just over a third said they knew their neighbours very well (26.5 per cent) or were close friends (8.6 per cent), under a third (28.6 per cent) said 'fairly well' and another third that they knew their neighbours 'only to say hello' (29.7 per cent), or 'not at all' (6.5 per cent).

The follow up survey interviewed 67 parish residents recruited by a networking process starting from contacts suggested by voluntary sector and church workers in the area. The sample cannot be taken as representative and it is particularly obvious that the Asian communities of the borough were not included in this research. The difficulties encountered during this snowball sampling procedure showed that for many people the number and strength of their local network ties was extremely limited. The fieldwork problems seemed to centre around the low level of trust of strangers, in the form of interviewers.

- Nearly 70 per cent liked living in the neighbourhood, but only 11 per cent saw it as a strong friendly community and only a third belonged to more than one community group.
- When asked to list up to 6 significant others in each category, respondents reported they were in touch with an average of 3.6 kin (outside their own household), 3.3 friends, and 2.9 neighbours. Older respondents had considerably more kin and neighbours, but less friends than younger respondents.
- Only a third of the relatives mentioned were living in Newham, compared with 70 per cent of the friends. Only 37 per cent of the relatives were seen at least weekly.
- Friends were likely to be of the same gender, and age group as the respondent. Inter-ethnic friendship was rare and almost unheard of among the older respondents.
- Neighbours seemed relatively insignificant to most people and only 10 per cent of the ones mentioned ever came inside the respondent's home.
- Over half the respondents felt they could turn to relatives and/or friends for routine help or support of more than one type, compared with only 20 per cent who could turn to neighbours. Even for the proverbial 'borrowing a cup of sugar' less than one in five had recently been helped by a neighbour and only another one in five thought they could approach a neighbour.

While it is hard to generalise about levels of social capital from this limited piece of research it does suggest some hypotheses which could be usefully investigated in future larger scale research. In this sample of respondents levels of social capital appeared to be rather low. Most of their investment was in a small number of close, private relationships, with help and support coming potentially and actually from relatives and friends. These relationships in many cases are hard to maintain because of geographical mobility and separation by distance. Lower levels of involvement with neighbours suggest a level of distrust of others in the public world. There appears to be little evidence of people investing in a wide range of 'weak ties' which according to Granovetter (1973) are especially useful in achieving economic and social goals. There are obvious contrasts too with the picture of the local community of Bethnal Green portrayed in Young and Wilmott (1957). For older respondents in the survey memories of a richer community life, and the experience of rapid neighbourhood change has left a sense of loss and grief, which may be explained to some extent by the findings of this research.

FAMILIES AND HOUSEHOLDS

A final set of data which may throw some light on the measurement of social capital relates to family and household structure. Broadly the argument is that people who live alone will have less dense networks of close supportive relationships than those who live in larger households and within families. The same may hold for families headed by lone parents in comparison with those where two parents are present. Single people and lone parent households are thus likely to possess less social capital than people in larger conventional families.

Clearly this argument can be contested both empirically and as ideology. It does seem likely, for example, that many people living alone may compensate for the lack of dense supportive networks by a more diffuse network comprising higher numbers of friends and acquaintances to whom they can turn. Likewise lone parents may have supportive networks in the form of extended family (including the 'absent' partner) and friends. It could be argued also that for some people at least being forced to live in the confines of a large family, possibly with overcrowding, stress and abusive relationships, should not be counted as a form of social capital. However, this should not blind us to the fact that stresses of other kinds affect many people living alone, and in lone parent families, and many individuals who are not in such situations entirely by choice, long for an end to loneliness, or for a stable 'conventional' family situation.

So with these provisos in mind we will present some selected data from the 1991 Census to help compare the family and household patterns found in Newham with those elsewhere.

In terms of adults living alone Newham has a considerable number. The proportion of such households ranges from 25 per cent in St. Stephens Ward (in Forest Gate) to 39 per cent in Ordnance Ward (Canning Town). However Newham stands out (especially the multi-ethnic Eastern part of the borough) as having low proportions of single person households compared with the rest of London. In many wards in West London boroughs single person households are a majority, in some as high as 80 per cent of all households and borough averages reach over 40 per cent in Westminster, Kensington and Chelsea, Brent and Hammersmith. However the other London East boroughs going outward have similar or slightly lower rates of lone person households to Newham, while the average for the UK is around 30 per cent.

For single parent households the picture for Newham is more ambivalent. The proportion of families comprising a lone parent and one or more dependent children reaches well over 20 per cent in three wards in Canning Town and Stratford, well towards the top of the league table for wards both in London and nationally. But again in the multi-ethnic east of Newham rates are generally about 10-15 per cent, around the average for London. The Newham average of 15.25 per cent is considerably lower than the 20 per cent found in boroughs such as Hackney, Islington, Southwark and Lambeth. The national average is about 14 per cent.

In terms of average numbers per household at the ward level Newham (together with Tower Hamlets, parts of North London and bordering areas of Redbridge) stands out as way above the London and national average. The mean number of persons per household is above 2.2 in every Newham ward and above 3.0 in four central wards of the borough. This borough average of 2.63 is substantially higher than that for all the other East London boroughs while elsewhere in the capital only Harrow and Brent reach a similar figure.

Clearly these patterns of household structure are linked with the multi-ethnic nature of Newham's populations, with many large and overcrowded households in the Asian and African communities. One would hazard a guess that insofar as family and community networks remain well established and functional for these communities, they could represent a potentially rich accumulation of social capital. Coming full circle back to the argument that social capital promotes economic prosperity, it might well be that the relative success of some of the ethnic minorities in business and education documented in a recent PSI report (Modood et al 1997) is explained at least in part by the strength of their social networks. In contrast the failure of the white, (and to some extent the black) non-working class in East London to achieve economic success can be linked to low levels, and possibly the historic erosion of social capital in their communities. There are obvious dangers in adopting this theory, without taking into account the overwhelming influence of global capitalism and the massive economic restructuring of East London. However, it is an interesting hypothesis around which a programme of further research could profitably be centred.

Conclusion

In this article I have argued that the notion of social capital is a useful one in evaluating the resources to be found in a place like Newham. It is, however, totally impossible and probably misguided to reduce the concept of social capital in its many varied forms to a single measurable index. It is also beyond the scope of any existing research project in East London to make statistically valid, comparative or longitudinal conclusions. Nonetheless, it has been possible to investigate the nature and extent of social capital as a by-product of existing community and voluntary sector studies. However imperfect this evidence and the measures suggested, they could provide a baseline against which to measure the growth or decline of social capital in the borough in coming years.

The overall weight of the evidence presented here, drawn from a variety of community-based research projects, coupled with years of experience as a community worker and active citizen in Newham is ambivalent. Do we say as optimists that the glass is half full or as pessimists that it is half empty? Studies of the general public suggest that for many if not most local people, economic deprivation compounded by lack of human capital (educational and skills resources) is matched by low levels of accumulation of social capital. It is worth asking again if there is a causal link. More rigorous research to check this out would be well worthwhile. Certainly for the poorest people in Newham participation in public life, and the number and depth of personal supportive relationships is at a low level and may well be declining. This is at the heart of social exclusion or marginalisation.

However, there is within Newham another side of the story. The voluntary sector has a huge range of organisations and community groups serving every conceivable sector and interest group. The religious communities are alive and growing, and involve as many as a third of the population in their activities. Religious organisations are a key factor in the networking of ethnic minority communities. The network structures of the voluntary sector provide many useful channels for information sharing and support. All this presents a massive resource of social capital for the community as a whole. The voluntary/community/religious sector offers major opportunities for community and economic development, in partnership with the local authority and other agencies in the private and public sector. It can also serve as a counterweight and 'opposition' to the concentration of power in the hands of a political elite.

In order to maximise the accumulation, and ensure a more equitable distribution of social capital for the public good two major problems need to be addressed. The first is wider participation, a key issue in any attempt to make democracy work. We have suggested, although the evidence is anecdotal rather than conclusive, that many of the voluntary sector community groups are self appointed and self-perpetuating organisations. In many cases they are doing a competent professional job, yet are based on a tiny active membership, and often linked together in the relatively closed networks that constitute the sector and the Newham establishment. Public sector consultation exercises turn out to be conversations with these unrepresentative activist elites. It seems unlikely that these few social capitalists can properly represent the interests of, or even ensure the welfare of, the social proletariat of Newham. Even with the political will and the effective implementation of the best community development techniques, in which informal rather than bureaucratic relationship building would need to take centre stage, it will be a hard long-term struggle to raise participation levels.

The second problem is the potential for fragmentation and conflict. Newham is already a uniquely diverse community, with a majority of minorities in its populations. In a region facing major economic and social stress, high levels of social exclusion, and urban regeneration and restructuring of the economy on a massive scale, the potential for conflict and even social disintegration is high. A well-resourced programme of investment in the *social* infrastructure would seem essential. The concept of social infrastructure would need to be a broad one which recognised the reality of pluralism and multiple special interests but would aim to bridge the multifarious divisions in the borough and to distribute its energies and resources fairly across the many distinctive groups. Only then can the high hopes for economic regeneration and the positive contribution of multiculturalism in the region have much chance of success.

The final word must be about the need to integrate the development of a stakeholder society with a stakeholder economy. Almost regardless of the truth or otherwise of Putnam's theory of the link between social capital and economic prosperity, it seems breathtakingly obvious on the basis of any values that seek the welfare of the people of East London, that the majority would benefit from a bigger stake in the national economy. The mechanisms of this problem of distribution are not our concern here but it is at least plausible that greater economic inclusion could have positive social consequences. Equally it seems that increased reserves of social capital well distributed through the local population would make the region a better place, more precisely a more human and humane community in which to live. However, for maximum benefit, the social, economic, and indeed the cultural resources ought to come together in synergy, which leads one suggests if somewhat tentatively , that some measure of social ownership, or at least communitarian or co-operative stakeholding in the economy is an appropriate way forward. Whether these ideas are anything other than unrealistically utopian in the face of global capitalism and the march of the individualistic consumer culture of our age, time alone will tell.

I wish to thank my colleagues at Aston Community Involvement Unit who have contributed to the research programme on which this paper is based, in particular Anne Crisp, Hazel Aimey and two groups of students from the London Hospital Medical College at QMW, who undertook most of the fieldwork for the surveys. Thanks also to Mike Locke and Steven Howlett of the Centre for Institutional Studies at UEL, John Williamson and an anonymous referee who read and made comments on an early draft of the paper.

Greg Smith can be contacted at CREDO, Mayflower Family Centre, Vincent Street, London E16 1LZ or by email as greg3@uel.ac.uk.

REFERENCES

Abrams, P. and M. Bulmer (1986), *Neighbours, the work of Philip Abrams*, Cambridge: Cambridge University Press

Alinsky, S. (1972), *Rules for Radicals*, New York: Vintage Books.

ACUPA (1985), *Faith in the City*, London: Church House Publishing.

Aston CIU, (1994), *Newham Directory of Religious Groups*, (Second Edition) available from CIU, Durning Hall, London E7 9AB (œ5).

Bourdieu, P.(1972), *Esquisse d'une theorie de la pratique. Precedee de trois etudes d'ethnologie kabyle*, Geneve: Droz, 227-243.

Burkett and Ashton (1996), The birth of the stakeholder society, *Critical Social Policy*, vol. 16 (4), pp3-16.

Coleman, J. (1990), *Foundations of Social Theory*, Harvard: Harvard University Press.

Crisp, A. and G. Smith (1997), *Valuable Resources: young people and services provided for them in Newham*. Report for Newham Safer Cities Project (full and summary versions available for £5 from Aston CIU, Durning Hall, London E7 9AB).

Dangschat, J. (1994), Concentration of poverty in the landscapes of boomtown Hamburg - the creation of a new urban underclass, *Urban Studies*, Vol. 31(7), 1133-1147.

Department of Environment, (1994), *Index of Local Conditions; an analysis based on 1991 Census Data*, London: HMSO.

Edwards, B. and M.W. Foley (1997), Social capital and the political economy of our discontent, *American Behavioral Scientist*, Vol. 40(5), 669-678.

Etzioni, A. (1994), *The Spirit of Community: the reinvention of American society*, New York: Touchstone/Simon and Schuster.

Farnell, R., S. Lund, R. Furbey, P. Lawless and B. Wishart, (1994a), *Broad Based Organising; An Evaluation For The Church Urban Fund*, CRESR: Sheffield Hallam University.

FOE/NEF (1997), *More isn't always better; a special briefing on growth and quality of life in the UK*, London: Friends of the Earth and New Economics Foundation (1ˢᵗ floor Vine Court, 112 Whitechapel Road, E1 1JE).

Foley, M.W. and B. Edwards (1997), Escape from politics? Social theory and the social capital debate, *American Behavioral Scientist*, Vol. 40(5), 550-561.

Freeman, L.C., A.K. Romney and D.R. White (1989), *Research Methods In Social Network Analysis*, Fairfax, Virginia: George Mason University Press.

Friedland, L.A. and J.M. McLeod (forthcoming), Community integration and mass media: a reconsideration, in Demers D.P and K. Viswanath (eds.), *Mass Media, Social Control and Social Change*.

Fukuyama, F. (1995), *Trust: The Social Virtues and the Creation of Prosperity*, New York: The Free Press.

Granovetter, M. (1973), The strength of weak ties, *American Journal of Sociology*, Vol. 78, pp1360-1380.

Greeley, A. (1997), Coleman revisited - religious structures as a source of social capital, *American Behavioral Scientist*, Vol. 40(5), 587-594.

Hanifan, L. J. (1920), *The Community Center*, Boston: Silver, Burdette and Co, 78-9.

Heying, C.H. (1997), Civic elites and corporate delocalization - an alternative explanation for declining civic engagement, *American Behavioral Scientist*, Vol. 40(5), 657-668.

Jacobs, J. (1961), *The Death and Life of Great American Cities*, Harmondsworth: Penguin Books.

Kenworthy, L. (1997), Civic engagement, social capital, and economic cooperation, *American Behavioral Scientist*, Vol. 40(5), 645-656.

Knight, B. and Stokes P. (1996), The Deficit in Civil Society in the United Kingdom, Working Paper No 1 of the Foundation for Civil Society, 200 Banbury Road, Birmingham B31 2DL.

Knight, B. (1993), *Voluntary Action*, London: Centris.

Kolankiewicz, G. (1996), Social capital and social-change, *British Journal of Sociology*, Vol. 47(3), 427-441.

Mai, U. (1997), Culture shock and identity in East German cities, in Oncu A. and Weyland P. (eds) (1997), *Space, Culture and Power: new identities in global cities*, London Zed Books.

Marchant, C. (1986), Religion, in *A Marsh and a Gas Works: one hundred years of life in West Ham*, W.E.A./Newham Parents Centre Publications, 745 Barking Road London E13 9ER.

Marriott, J. (1996) The political modernism of East London, in T. Butler and M. Rustin (eds), *Rising in the East? The regeneration of East London*, London: Lawrence & Wishart.

Minkoff, D.C. (1997), Producing social capital - National social movements and civil society, *American Behavioral Scientist*, Vol. 40(5), 606-6,

Mitlin, D. and J. Thomson (1995), Participatory approaches in urban areas: strengthening civil society or reinforcing the status quo? in *Environment And Urbanization*, Vol. 7(1), 231-250.

Modood, T. *et al* (1997), *Ethnic Minorities in Britain: Diversity and Disadvantage*, London: Policy Studies Institute.

Newton, K. (1997), Social capital and democracy, *American Behavioral Scientist*, Vol. 40(5), 575-586.

Norris, P. (1996), Does Television erode social capital - a reply to Putnam, *Political Science and Politics*, Vol. 29(3), 474-480.

Pahl, R. (1996), Social capital and social-change - comment, *British Journal of Sociology*, Vol. 47(3), 443-446.

Portney, K.E. and J.M. Berry (1997), Mobilizing minority communities - social capital and participation in urban neighborhoods, *American Behavioral Scientist*, Vol. 40(5), 632-644.

Putnam, R.D. (1993), *Making Democracy Work; Civic Traditions in Modern Italy*, Princeton New Jersey: Princeton University Press.

Putnam, R.D. (1995), Tuning in, tuning out - the strange disappearance of social capital in America, *Political Science and Politics*, Vol. 28(4), 664-683.

Reynolds, J., K.T. Elsdon and S. Stewart (1994), *A Town in Action; Voluntary Networks in Retford*, Dept. of Adult Education, University of Nottingham

Schumacher, E.F. (1973), *Small Is Beautiful, Economics As If People Mattered*, London: Blond and Briggs.

Schusterman, R. and A. Hardoy (1997), Reconstructing social capital in a poor urban settlement: the integral improvement programme in Barrio San Jorge, *Environment and Urbanization*, Vol. 9(1), 91-119.

Scott, J. (1992), *Social Network Analysis*, London, Sage.

Skelcher, C., A. McCabe, V. Lowndes and P. Nanton (1996), *Community Networks in Urban Regeneration: 'it all depends on who you know...!'* , Bristol: Polity Press/Joseph Rowntree Foundation.

Smith, G. (1992), *West Ham Parish Survey Report*, London: Aston Community Involvement Unit, London E7 9AB .

Smith, G. (1994), *Neighbourhood and Networks in Newham*, London: Aston Community Involvement Unit, Durning Hall, London E7 9AB.

Smith, G. (1996), The Unsecular City, The Revival Of Religion In East London, in T. Butler and M. Rustin (eds), *op cit.*

Smith, G, (1996b), Community-arianism, Published electronically. Available via the Internet at http://www.communities.com/greg/gsum.html or in hard copy from Aston CIU London E7 9AB.

Smith, G. (1997), Religious networks in a multicultural, multifaith setting, paper presented at ISSR Sociology of Religion conference, Toulouse, July 1997. (electronic version available by email from the author).

Smith, G. (1998), Mapping the voluntary and community sector, a network analysis in one London borough, in *Proceedings of NCVO Research Conference*, 3-5 September 1997, South Bank University, London, National Council for Voluntary Organisations.

Smith, G. (forthcoming), Religious belonging, ethnicity and inter faith encounter, *Journal of Contemporary Religion*. (An early version presented as a paper in April 1996 to the BSA Sociology of Religion Group Conference. Available by email from the author).

Wellman B. and B. Wellman (1992), Domestic affairs and network relations, in *Journal of Social and Personal Relationships*, London: Sage.

Wellman, B. (1979), The Community Question: the intimate networks of East Yorkers, in *American Journal of Sociology*, vol. 84(5), 1201-31.

Wellman, B. and S. Wortley (1990), Different strokes from different folks: community ties and social support, *American Journal of Sociology*, 96, 558 588.

Willmott, P. (1987), *Friendship Networks and Social Support*, London: Policy Studies Institute.

Willmott, P. (1986), *Social Networks, Informal Care and Public Policy*, PSI Research report 655, London: Policy Studies Institute.

Wilson, P.A. (1997), Building social capital: a learning agenda for the twenty-first century, *Urban Studies*, Vol. 34(5-6), 745-760.

Wood, R.L. (1997), Social capital and political culture - God meets politics in the inner city, *American Behavioral Scientist*, Vol. 40(5), pp. 595-605.

Young, M. and P. Wilmott (1957), *Family and Kinship in East London*, Harmondsworth: Penguin Books edition, 1962.

NOTES

1. I would like to acknowledge that the definitions and quotations used in the introductory section are derived from an open discussion on the SOCNET listserv which took place in June 1997 and was collated and reposted by by Michael Lichter. Among the key participants were Robert Putnam, Barry Wellman, Lewis Friedland and Xavier da Sousa Briggs. SOCNET (**SOCNET@NERVM.NERDC.UFL.EDU**) is a discussion list associated with INSNA, the International Network for social Network Analysis, and details of how to subscribe can be found on their web site: **http://www.heinz.cmu.edu/project/INSNA/.**

2. The LBN Social services 'Community Care Database'. Version 2.6 July 1997 on which the statistics on the local voluntary sector are based is available on disk from David Williamson LBN Social Services Broadway House, Stratford E15, (tel. 0181 534 4545) or on line in Newham Libraries, public information (ATTACH) kiosks, and the LBN web site (**http:www/newham/gov.uk).**

3. The Data analysis for this research was carried out using two software packages - *UCINET IV* by Borgatti Everett & Freeman Copyright Analytic Technologies 1994, and '*Krackplot 3.0* An improved network drawing program' by Krackhardt D., Blythe J & McGrath C. *Connections* Vol. 17.2 December 1994. Information from Krackplot web site **http://www.heinz.cmu.edu/~krack/index.html.**

4. Further details on this data and its interpretation is available from the author.

5. Statistics on UK parliamentary elections are taken from the Elections archive web site based at Queen Mary & Westfield College (**http://www.qmw.ac.uk/%7Elaws/election/index.html**). US election turnout data can be found on **http://www.fec.gov/pages/htm1to5.htm.**

6. Local election results were published in the Newham Recorder for the first week of May 1994.

Fossils and forests:

East London over the last sixty million years

Mike Boulter

Mike Boulter looks at some of the paleontological evidence of the last sixty million years, much of which comes from around East London, to put into context the changes that are beginning to occur in the global climate. These changes are nothing new, however this time the causes may be the consequences of human intervention in the natural world. We have been warned.

The time is fast approaching for East Londoners to feel especially involved with international events. With all the hype most of us know that the final century in the second Christian millennium is coming to an end. The international measure of time is closely connected to our planet's rhythms and the 0 degree longitude meridian at Greenwich is the standard (Sobel 1996). Jerusalem has one up on us in that Christ was born there a couple of thousand years ago (putting that date crudely as we must) but what most East Londoners don't know is that a lot of our knowledge of environmental change through the last 2,000 years, as well as the last 60,000,000 years, is based on evidence from within a few miles of Tower Bridge.

There is a lot of knowledge published in the scientific literature and I will summarise a little of that which I think is relevant and sympathetic to the topic. It is important to understand that this is a very small sample of what has been done about East London's history over the last 60 million years, and full justice to that effort would occupy a volume ten times the size of this. More important is the validity of this knowledge, its status as scientific value. You will see that some of the ideas presented are uncertain, expect them all to be questioned.

Part of the problem is that the concept of such long periods of time is difficult for most of us to comprehend (let alone establish): that people used to retire at an age precisely one millionth of the latter length of time is hard to conceive. One way is to make proportional analogies to well-known time periods, such as the 60 minutes of an hour being equivalent to the 60 million year period mentioned above. Within that hour each minute represents a million years and the 2,000 years of Christianity we celebrate soon would be about a tenth of a second. Other events on the one hour time scale are shown in Figure 1 in which the sixty minutes of an hour are compared to the last 60 million years. Of course, our units of time themselves are based on modern observations of our planet orbiting the sun. These orbital parameters have changed through time as the rate of rotation of the earth slows, the angle of incidence of the planet rises and falls, just as our orbit around the sun changes. Some of the consequences of these kinds of change are discussed in a very readable recent best seller *Longitude* (Sobel 1996).

We are getting to know the resulting changes to our environment rather well, but those of more than a few thousand years are still very difficult to detect. The best known are three types of cycle of 96,000, 42,000 and 21,000 years duration, thought by their discoverer Milankovitch to be caused by solar-orbit factors. These rhythms are increasingly notable in the global cooling that started about 23 million years ago (at the beginning of the Miocene Period) and reached a peak during the ice ages of the last one and a half million years (the last one and a half minutes on our clock - Figure 1).

The last two thousand years

Throughout these warm and cold phases East London was dominated by the rise and fall of the river and its delta, in turn influenced by the rise and fall in sea-level as the English Channel kept forming and breaking England's land connection to the European mainland. Indeed, the Thames, the Seine and the Rhine all fed the lowland of what is now the southern North Sea with each of the rivers' estuaries giving very varied maps of clear shorelines. For instance, not until the Thames river banks were built by the Victorians to stop flooding and create docks did firm land exist in East London. You can still see a small vestige of what the region must have been like up until the mid-nineteenth century as you travel on the North London Line between Hackney Wick and Stratford. The train crosses the tidal (up to 7 metres) River Lea a few metres north of the triangle-shaped railway junction to the east. The area inside the triangle is protected by the track from the highest tides of the nearby river, though it is still low-lying and comprises freshwater swamp with reed-burr and sedges. Without the protection of the railway this low-lying land would be marsh, controlled by the tides of the river and

Figure 1. A one-hour time scale for 60 million years. The intervals of time mentioned in this article revolve clockwise. The names of geological periods and events are mentioned in the text. (Ma = million years ago)

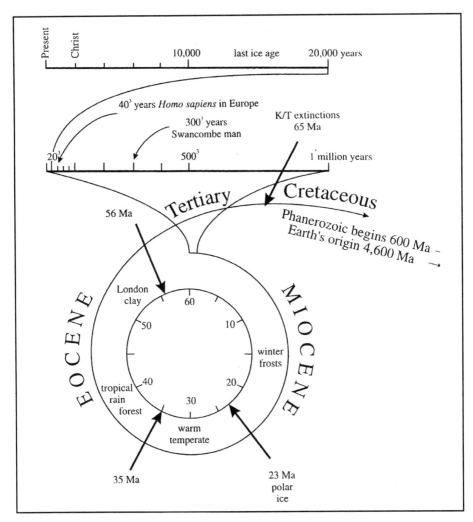

the currents of the estuary itself. That is what most of the area of what is now East London looked like a few hundred years ago!

This picture of low-lying land dominated by tides and changes in sea level was similar all around what is now the Thames estuary. In London, the further west the river went the higher the flood plain and the firmer the river banks. When these were not clear the consequent marshland would have been fresh-water with an ecosystem similar to that of many East Anglia fens.

The impact of local ice ages

The eventual consequence of the Milankovitch cycles was the formation of ice caps on our planet. Through the last 600 million years (ten hours of our 60 minute clock) the earth only had polar ice twice, each time for just a few million years (a few minutes, twice, in those ten hours). It was much more usual for the poles to have a temperate climate and the range of temperature down to the equator was much less varied than now. At its coldest, the ice from the north reached as far south as the Thames valley and one of the most southerly terminal moraines forms the hill just north of East Finchley underground station. It was by such great movements of glacial debris that the river Thames is established in its present position. During this time of the Ice Age London was glaciated and covered with perma-frost several times, alternating with intervals of temperate and even warm-temperate interglacials. The Thames estuary has always been an important refuge to help preserve the evidence of these changes. Not only does it mark the most southern extent of glaciation but its sediments contain records of environmental and biological changes through the time of deposition. Although the river sands and gravels comprising its terraces contain only limited evidence, the clay and mudstones found from more tranquil climes do contain abundant and fascinating material. One of the most famous collections of fossils from perhaps the warmest interglacial was found last century when the fountains and street architecture of Trafalgar Square were being built. This 'Trafalgar Square Interglacial' deposit yielded bones of elephant, mammoth, etc which are on display in the galleries at the Natural History Museum.

There, you will also see another local fauna from an interglacial period and exhibits of another local fauna from the last interglacial, including a skulls of a *Homo erectus* from Swanscombe in Kent variously dated at betweem 200,000 and 450,000 years. The relationship of these skulls from south of the river to the standard types of that species and to those of Neanderthal man are highly controversial and many specialists disagree about important details. It is difficult to be sure about the age, the morphological interpretations of often badly preserved bones, let alone the relationship to the closest similar specimens from Wales and France

East London's tropical rain forest

The period of time between 35 and 56 million years ago, the Eocene, is represented in East London by some of the best known sediments such as the London Clay (Collinson, 1983). Throughout this time the level of the North Sea kept rising and falling, maybe due to something like Milankovitch cycles, and, respectively, this caused marine transgressions (floods) and marine regressions (land). You can find evidence of these changes over most of East London, in exposures near streams and cuttings, boreholes, and most famously on the north-east facing cliffs on the Isle of Sheppey.

The climate of the environments producing these sediments was very different to those of the ice ages. As our clock goes backwards from the ice ages at two minutes to the hour, high latitudes warm considerably, so that at half past the hour (30Ma) East London had a very warm temperate climate. Earlier still, about 37 million years ago, the temperatures were at their maxima and we see evidence of tropical rain forest flora and fauna from our local London Clay. This time is known as the Terminal Eocene Event and was first recognised by Buchardt (1982) with the discovery of tropical shellfish from sediments of this age in the North Sea. A few years later this laboratory here identified lianas and tropical rain forest trees as pollen in 37 million year old sediments just above the London Clay (Hubbard and Boulter 1985; Collinson, Fowler and Boulter, 1985).

To the east of London there is one further source of evidence which gives a fascinating and popular story. By the shoreline at Harwich, in Essex, there is a foreshore exposure known to be roughly 65 million years old (5 minutes beyond the range of our proportional clock). This represents the famous Cretaceous/Tertiary boundary which marks the event of a 20km diameter object from outer space hitting the earth, possibly causing many years of fire and darkness leading to the extinction of dinosaurs and many other animals. It hit Mexico but all north hemisphere localities of that age pick up some of the damage. The Harwich exposure shows ash and glass from the impact cloud.

Some consequences of this past for the present

'So what, about all these reconstructions from the every distant past?' you may say, 'What do they mean to us in the way we run our lives now?' There are several pathways to follow with your thinking, all concerned with the controversial principle that present physical features have historical precedents.

From what we can see of East London's archive of the last 60 million years, climate change is taking place continuously in cycles. Although global warming has advanced unnaturally quickly over the last 100 years, East London has had much higher temperatures. Carbon dioxide levels have also been much higher than the present artificially rising concentrations. Similarly, the Thames Barrier was constructed to protect London from what were unusually high tides, thought by many to be the direct cause of global warming from man's recent high standard of living. But we have evidence of previous changes in sea level at the Thames estuary many tens of thousands and millions of years ago. Although the rate of change is unnatural even higher levels have existed in the past.

The more I study and read around these ancient environmental changes the more I learn a high respect for ecological systems, and at the same time I expect them to change. Studying past environments gives a confident attitude to the agents of change by understanding what has happened earlier. The circumstances are different but the consequences may be the same. Natural systems must be allowed to relax into their own rhythms.

Another attitude this work encourages is to put our lifespan in a natural context. Most of us have difficulty thinking about intervals of time longer than a decade or two. Two thousand, or even twenty million years, are something else, though here it is essential and commonplace. The implications of this contrast are frightening (Moore *et al*, 1996). In the five decades of my own life the rate of change in the environment is rising increasingly quickly. The many different kinds of change in East London over the past 60 million years have been more extreme but have happened very much slower. So we are living through an environmental catastrophe such as the planet, let alone East London, has not known. Perhaps the most recent comparable shock to the planet occurred 65 million years ago when years of constant darkness caused the dinosaurs to become extinct. There is not long to go before a human-made catastrophe happens of comparable proportions. I believe it has started already.

REFERENCES

Buchardt, B. (1978) Oxygen isotope palaeotemperatures from the Tertiary period in the North Sea area. *Nature* 275, pp121-3.

Collinson, M.E. (1983) *Fossil Plants of the London Clay*. London: Palaeontological Association.

Collinson, M.E., K. Fowler and M.C. Boulter (1981), Floristic changes indicate a cooling climate in the Eocene of southern England, *Nature*: 291 315-7.

Fossils and forests

Duff, K.L. (ed) (1985), *The Story of Swanscombe Man*, Kent County Council and NCC.

Hubbard, R.N.L.B. and M.C. Boulter (1983), Reconstruction of Palaeogene climate from palynological evidence, *Nature* 301: 147-50.

Moore, P.D., W.G. Chaloner and P. Stott (1996), *Global Environmental Change*, Oxford: Blackwell.

Sobel, D. (1996) *Longitude*, London: Fourth Estate.

Gay men and the regeneration of an East London borough

Gavin Brown

Gavin Brown explores why Tower Hamlets has attracted a sizeable gay population and considers what this tells us about the spatial organisation of gay men's urban lives in East London. The article also proposes some ways in which the gay presence in the borough could contribute to the regeneration process.

Walking around Sainsbury's in Whitechapel on any evening or during the weekend, the 'knowing' eye will observe a disproportionately large number of gay men - single men quietly cruising each other, hoping to pick up more than a few groceries; couples bickering over how to spend their reward points; and large gaggles of friends busily preparing for a Sunday night feast in front of the TV and 'The Lily Savage Show'.

Over the last fifteen years or so, Tower Hamlets has become the home to a large and visible gay male population. This visibility is expressed primarily in two ways: the relatively large number of commercial venues and support services in the borough, and through the participation of gay men in the gentrification of the area. The commercial venues mentioned above form part of an arc that runs from Clerkenwell in the west through to Bethnal Green and Mile End in the east. At the centre of this arc is a cluster of half a dozen bars, three gay-orientated shops and a sauna on the edge of the City of London, around Shoreditch, most of which are not actually in Tower Hamlets, but just over the border in Hackney. I have chosen to include these venues in my discussion, as they are just a short walk from areas of Bethnal Green where many gay men live, and so to exclude them from my considerations would be as artificial and arbitrary as the local government boundaries themselves. However, there are also a significant number of venues in the borough itself. Along the course of Bethnal Green Road (and in the side streets off it) are another five bars and a restaurant. Further south, between

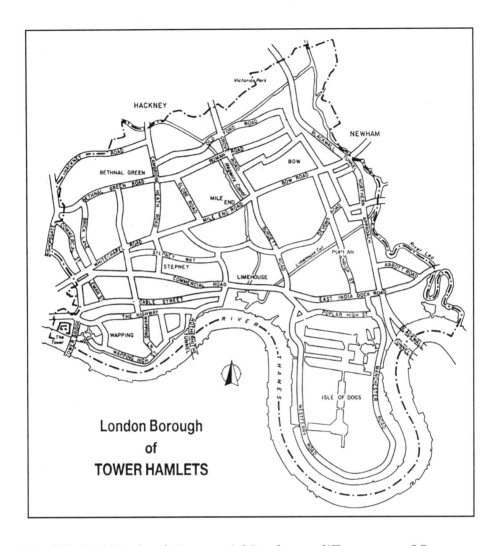

London Borough
of
TOWER HAMLETS

the Mile End Road and Commercial Road are a diffuse group of five more bars, a transvestite club, another sauna and the Globe Centre for people with HIV and AIDS. And finally, to the east near Mile End station are two long-running clubs, Benjys 2000 on a Sunday night (a gay East End institution) and The Backstreet, which claims to bring a bit of Amsterdam to London's East End.

An increasing volume of work has been written about the spatial organisation of gay men and women's urban lives (Castells and Murphy 1982; Knopp 1992; Bell and Valentine *et al*, 1995) but much of this has focused on gay life in North American cities. Of the work that has explored the development of gay enclaves in British cities, a substantial amount has been written about the growth in Manchester's 'Gay Village' and the concentration of gay businesses around Old Compton Street in London's Soho (Whittle 1994; Mort 1995; Quilley 1997). While both these areas are, in their own ways, quintessentially English, they follow a fairly international model of city centre gay districts, and have as much in common with areas of Amsterdam, San Francisco and Sydney as they do with other gay neighbourhoods in the British Isles. This article will attempt to begin to redress that balance, by exploring how the national and local political economy in East London has attracted, shaped and sustained a significant local gay population in the Tower Hamlets area.

I shall attempt to explain why a large number of gay men have chosen to live in Tower Hamlets, rather than other areas of the capital. In concentrating on the presence of a sizeable number of gay men in the area, I do not wish to suggest that there are no lesbians living in the borough or to further contribute to their invisibility, merely to recognise that the area has proved less enticing as a residential and recreational location for gay women and to explore some reasons for this. As I explain in the first section of the article, Tower Hamlets has sustained a working-class gay subculture for much of this century, and so the area's gay presence can be said to pre-date the internationalisation of gay culture that has taken place since the late 1960s (although this, as well as broader shifts in the international political economy, have undoubtedly had their effect the local gay population). The main focus of this article is a consideration of how, in a British context, gay men have utilised space in different ways to find a means of expressing their sexuality within the urban environment. Through this discussion I shall also examine the contribution that the borough's gay population and businesses have made to the regeneration of the area to date, and their needs and potential future input into this continuing process.

Perhaps, before I continue, it will be useful to pause a moment for a word about the language I will use throughout this article, in order to avoid future confusion. The discerning reader will have already noticed that I have so far avoided the phrase 'gay community'. This is deliberate. These two words have been greatly overused by gay activists and other commentators since the early 1970s, and suggest a social and political cohesion based on sexual preference that, as I believe this study will demonstrate, simply doesn't exist most of the time. I prefer the phrase 'gay population', although this too is less than perfect, and I hope readers will appreciate, by the end of the article, that I perceive this population to be shifting in size, membership and location across time and space. The gay population in Tower Hamlets is certainly fractured, in large part, along lines of race, class and gender. Rather than attempt to record a spectrum of essentialised 'ideal types', I am interested in identifying the various social forces that impact on these varied understandings of sexual identity, and the range of spatial strategies through which they are expressed.

When I use the terms 'lesbian', 'gay' and 'bisexual' I am generally referring to men and women who are open about their sexuality in most (if not all) aspects of their lives and for whom their sexuality plays an important role in defining their sense of self. At various points in the text, I will have reason to discuss men and women who periodically engage in homosexual activity, but who do not perceive such acts to be central to their sense of identity; to describe these people I shall either use the term 'homosexually-orientated men', or the less medicalised, but slightly wordy, phrase 'men who have sex with men'. Finally, on the occasions when I wish to refer to all those sexual dissidents who resist heteronormative constraints I shall use the term 'queer' as it is commonly understood in the twin spheres of academe and activism.

I shall begin this article with a brief history of the queer presence in the borough and demonstrate how, as queer people have seldom been able to express their sexuality uniformly in every sphere of their lives, specific sites have always played a significant role in shaping how gay sexuality is understood. In the second section of the article I shall consider the varying ways in which gay people have utilised different sites and spaces to express their sexuality and to find support and solidarity in an often hostile world. The third and fourth sections of the article explore in more depth how queer people from different ethnic and class backgrounds have utilised the urban landscape: from brief encounters in semi-public places to more lasting involvement in the property market. Finally, I shall return to the issue of the regeneration of East London and propose some ways in which the gay presence in Tower Hamlets can best contribute to this process.

The history of queer spaces in Tower Hamlets

I do not believe that it is possible to understand why a significant number of gay men have chosen to live in Tower Hamlets without examining the history of the queer presence in the area. For at least two centuries, the area's location on the edge of the City, and the presence of the docks and a large, shifting immigrant community has made Tower Hamlets an ideal home for those on the fringes of urban society (Norton 1992; Widgery 1993).

In the post-war decades preceding the partial decriminalisation of homosexuality, the docks sustained a number of working-class drag pubs that were in stark contrast to the more 'theatrical' gay haunts of Soho. Paul

Barlow, formerly the convenor of the Lesbian and Gay Workers Group at Tower Hamlets Council, explains:

> Did you want to know a bit about the history? A lot of people have pointed to the docks. There were a lot of gay pubs around the docks and they were really dark and dingy. I don't think there are any left that were servicing the sailors and dockers. The pubs are still standing, but they're obviously not still doing that. There was a pub called Charlie Brown's in Limehouse, which was the big, main drag venue. And that was something that was common in lots of East End pubs anyway, gay and straight. But also there were bars within pubs that had been gay for ages (one of our councillors told me about it, he's about 80 now). But there's always been a sort of working-class gay tradition in Tower Hamlets - it's always been a lot more tolerant in East London than people assume.

That the docks sustained a working-class gay subculture is not unique to the East End of London, but is a phenomenon that has been recorded in New York, San Francisco and other sea trading cities the world over (Castells and Murphy 1982; Chaucey 1994).

But the East End drag pubs were not the only way that what is now the borough of Tower Hamlets made its mark on the developing British gay subculture. From the eighteenth century onwards the area has supplied a steady stream of young men who have chosen to prostitute themselves in the West End, either out of economic necessity or as a means of entry into the predominantly middle-class homosexual subculture located there (Norton, 1992). While this is true of other working-class districts of London, the 'East End lad' has retained a particular place in the British gay erotic imagination. A quick trawl through the gay novels lying around my flat threw up at least four (including one published in the USA) that extolled the apparent sexual prowess of the rough East End lad. Similarly, a glance through the personal ads and the listings for gay sex lines in the back of most issues of *Boyz*, the weekly free paper of the young London gay scene, demonstrates just how deeply this sexual stereotype has been ingrained in our collective imagination: 'Gobbling Geezers East End Style 0896 4** ***' (*Boyz 334*, 6 December 1997)

Perhaps the best example I have come across is a personal ad quoted by Murray Healy (1996) from 3 July 1993:

> Rough but friendly, uncut, East End thug wanted by likeable 39 year old. Your mean attitude is my dream. Make it reality. Come and frighten me into submission with your anger, please.

Given the extent to which gay male residential concentrations in much of the

West tend to develop in close proximity to the sexual marketplace, the imaginary role of East End 'rough trade' cannot be discounted from our consideration of why gay men have moved to the Tower Hamlets area.

Having considered the cultural history of the gay male presence in the borough, it is worth exploring briefly the politics of the gay East End. For a period of about six months in 1973 members of the Gay Liberation Front ran a commune on Bethnal Green Road, 'Bethnal Rouge'. The choice of the East End as a site for this commune seems to have been largely a happy accident; but the GLF had previously consciously chosen to hold one of their Gay Day picnics in the borough's Victoria Park, in order to take their political work into a working-class district. Nearly twenty-five years later, Victoria Park was the scene of a far larger 'gay day', when it was the site for the 1995 Pride Festival.

Despite the GLF's periodic work in the area and the working-class drag tradition, in the 1980s Tower Hamlets, unlike the London boroughs of Hackney, Haringey and Lambeth, never really acquired a reputation in the popular imagination as a gay-friendly borough. With the Liberals controlling the town hall during the period 1986-94, the borough was never smeared with the 'loony-left' council label that was applied to so many other Inner London boroughs by the tabloid press in the mid-to-late 1980s, in which racism and anti-gay prejudice were fully utilised to try and destabilise the left reformist programmes of many municipal Labour councils. This example demonstrates how social and political discourses can contribute to our understanding of specific spaces within the city; in the next section of this article, I shall explore further the connection between the social and spatial sphere in shaping our perceptions of different sites.

Sexuality, identity and space

In recent years an increasing number of geographers and scholars from other fields have begun to consider the material and imaginary ways in which queer people utilise specific sites, and the spatial field more generally, to construct and consolidate their sense of identity. Harvey (1989) and Knopp (1992) have both emphasised the connection between culture (and sexuality) and class interests, arguing that the cultural and sexual coding of a neighbourhood can be an important element in defining an area's image and that this in turn has come to play a central role in the process of capital accumulation, the reproduction of social relations and the very way in which space in produced and transformed. Urban design from the nineteenth century onwards has produced and reproduced a built environment that presumes and reproduces through the design of its neighbourhoods, homes, workplaces and leisure venues a gender-based spatial division of labour that is dominantly heterosexual and experienced through an understanding of distinct public and private spheres. Although urban space is often presumed to be heterosexual, it can be 'queered' in any number of ways, from the passing acts of kissing, holding hands or having sex in public places, to a gay couple or group of friends setting up home together. I believe it is useful and constructive to engage with these debates in order to fully understand and describe the queer presence in Tower Hamlets, exploring the varying ways in which issues of race, class and gender affect the use of space by queer people from different social backgrounds.

A number of commentators (Johnston and Valentine 1995; Jay 1997) have argued that to centre an evaluation of queer territoriality on concentrations of commercial venues and home ownership is to privilege the experience of professional, often white, gay men. Due to the wider socio-economic disadvantages faced by women, lesbians often do not chose to live in gay enclaves, but rather prioritise 'home' and supportive social networks that are often more spatially diverse. As Paul Barlow comments:

> The obvious thing is that Tower Hamlets is very gay male. Hackney is very lesbian; and that's an economic thing to do with the cost of housing.

While the gender-related economic issue raised by Paul Barlow should not be underestimated, the reality of the housing markets in the two boroughs is more complex than might at first be inferred from his comments: despite concentrations of expensive residential properties in Bow and some areas of Docklands, average property values are probably lower in Tower Hamlets than in Hackney. Hackney does, however, have something of a reputation as a trendy and slightly bohemian area and it is worth considering in this context the lasting impact of lesbian feminism, which has encouraged some lesbians to orientate towards areas linked with the countercultural milieu rather than the sexual marketplaces associated with so many gay male enclaves (Bouthillette 1997). Tamar Rothenburg (1995) recognises that the discrepancies between male and female wages can mitigate against lesbians making a significant impact in the gentrification of inner city areas, but she challenges the assumption that lesbians have played no role in this process, suggesting instead that they may be attracted to areas where properties are cheaper, therefore, often opening them up to new waves of gentrification. If women's economic disadvantages reduce their options in the residential property market, they are also less likely to own their own business, which may help explain why lesbian enclaves often leave less impact on the urban landscape in terms of the presence of commercial venues and service organisations.

It is important to remember that, as gay people, we do not simply choose our friends and neighbourhoods on the basis of our sexuality - social class, the location of our work, religion, care responsibilities and a host of other factors all impact on our daily lives and the way we perceive our identities. Gay people are not born into a 'gay community'; we make a conscious decision to assert our identities, and thus, to some extent construct those identities. This is also true of gay neighbourhoods. Although significant gay subcultures have existed periodically in Europe and North American since the late nineteenth century, gay 'communities', as they are currently understood in the West, have a relatively short history developing only since the birth of the modern gay liberation movement in the late 1960s. As a result, gay people, perhaps more than other social groups with greater historical resources, have less tradition to work from in constructing their spaces, so our material and cultural landscape is continually being produced and reproduced.

David Bell and Gill Valentine (1995) argue that the 'heterosexing' of most urban spaces is a performative act that is naturalised through repetition. Building on the work of Judith Butler on the role of performativity in constructing both self and space as prediscursively straight, they identify the potential for subversive spatial acts to disrupt the previously seamless space of heterosexuality. This conceptual framework is useful if we are to explore the full range of queer spaces in the contemporary city. Unlike the location of commercial gay venues or areas of gay gentrification, bisexual and transgendered spaces are harder to locate on the urban map, as they are created far more by the performativity of the body in the landscape than by property relations.

Gay spaces have many facets: economic and political, as well as social and psychological; and their formation is an act that confronts and transgresses the boundaries of culturally enforced heterosexuality. As the editors of *Queers in Space* note, 'Identifying a place as queer is a deliberate action parallel to "coming out"'(Ingram, Bouthillette & Retter, 1997). While the example of Tower Hamlets clearly highlights the existence of a working class gay subculture throughout much of this century, there is a large extent to which creating a stable, supportive and desirable queer space in the public domain is still very much the preserve of the affluent and socially privileged.

In city centre gay areas, such as Old Compton Street in Soho, there has been a move away from the 'dubious bar' as a place for socialising, to a more diverse set of social spaces and places of consumption, such as cafes, boutiques, gyms and book shops. In Tower Hamlets the old-fashioned, dubious bar behind blacked out windows is still very much in evidence. Paul Barlow has a theory:

> A lot of pubs are closing down in East London, a lot are being converted into other businesses, and one option for a lot of pub-owners is to turn it into a gay pub. ... and they're probably pubs that would have closed down otherwise. But no-one has invested any money in them. ... And the really dark and dingy ones tend to be the working-class bars. ... There's obviously an issue around poverty; and the people who tend to live on the estates use those more than the people on the private estates, who tend to go into town.

If this is the case for the less affluent, but relatively settled, sections of urban society, it is even more the case for those who are most marginalised by poverty, racism and anti-gay sentiment. For them, the 'queerness' of the sites through which they find a means to express their sexuality can be very fleeting indeed and it is the experience of these men that I shall explore in the next section of this article.

Marginalised queers

There is an assumption in much of what I have written so far that the gay men under discussion are, to one extent or another, open about their sexuality in many spheres of their lives. However, such men only constitute a minority of men who have sex with other men.

Those men who have sex, however frequently, with members of their own sex, come from across the social spectrum. However, as white men from all social classes, along with smaller numbers of Afro-Caribbean and South-East Asian men, participate in the commercial gay scene in Tower Hamlets, for the purposes of this study, and in order to best reflect the demography of the borough, I shall concentrate my discussion of marginalised homosexualities by examining the experience of homosexually-orientated men of Bangladeshi heritage. Many of the issues raised below are pertinent to men of any social background who either do not perceive themselves as gay (or bisexual) or who for economic (or other reasons) have little contact with the gay scene. Given the existence of a working-class gay subculture in Tower Hamlets over a number of decades, however, the experience of queer Bangladeshi men contrasts most vividly with that of the borough's white, middle-class gay gentrifiers.

There are a number of easily identified reasons why homosexually-oriented Bangladeshis might choose not to participate in the commercial gay scene, even if they identify as gay or bisexual. These range from the cultural and religious attitudes to homosexuality within the Bangladeshi community, economic and language barriers, 'misreadings' of the popular gay skinhead style, and the centrality of alcohol consumption to most commercial gay venues.

For those who are economically unable to live independently of the family unit (or whose culture discourages this practice), the possibilities of leading a fully rounded gay existence are severely restricted. Most government reports and legislation since the Wolfenden Report which led to the partial decriminalisation of homosexuality have encouraged the privatisation of homosexuality based largely on private ownership of property. But for those who do not have access to this level of privacy, for whatever reason, there are few options but to find space to satisfy their (homo)sexual needs in the public domain. Given the centrality of the extended family network in many South Asian cultures, within which eurocentric notions of privacy and public space do not necessarily apply, this is especially likely to be the case for Bangladeshi men who have sex with men.

With the extended family continuing to play such a pivotal role, partly as a means of protection and solidarity against the racism of British society, marriage and the rearing of children take on enormous significance and the importance of upholding family honour is central. Within the extended family, an individual's primary duty is to the maintenance of family honour, with individual choice and personal rights frequently subsumed to this. As a result, to go against the family in order to lead a gay existence can mean losing far more than might be the case in a white British context; it can mean losing touch not only with one's family, but also with an important aspect of what it means to be Asian.

In his work on the sexual health needs of South Asian men, Shivananda Khan (1991) has argued that it is unhelpful to apply western categories of sexual identity to South Asian men who have sex with other men; in part, because adequate terms to describe such experiences or identities do not exist in most South Asian languages. But he also argues that, in the context of the South Asian diaspora, gender segregation, the low status of women, a strong sense of duty and honour to the extended family and greater male homosociability all contribute to a situation in which large numbers of men participate in male to male sex. Often, this is for entirely opportunistic reasons - the men concerned may not even question their (hetero)sexuality and are purely taking advantage of the possibility of quick, uncomplicated sexual release. When I asked his views on this, Shahidul Miah, of the Tower Hamlets Equalities Unit, replied with a laugh, 'Oh yeah, it's rampant!'.

For those who do wish to mix with other South Asian queers, there is the support group Shakti, and a monthly club night, Club Kali. Because these events are organised by and for South Asian men and women, they have the advantage of providing a supportive space away from the pressures of both the extended family and racist society. For Bangladeshi men and women from the East End, they also have the added advantage of taking place elsewhere in London and so a safe distance can be kept between their familial obligations and their 'gay' lives.

To date there has been very little work done in Tower Hamlets with queer men of Bangladeshi heritage. While Streetwise Youth did carry out a study of Bangladeshi male prostitution in the area, this is reported to have come to very little. So, such men, discouraged from using local commercial venues, as much out of fear of disclosure, as for the other reasons outlined above, will continue to find a sexual outlet in the public sphere: in public toilets ('cottages'), parks and the growing number of saunas opening up in the area and around London. This is not to suggest that only Bangladeshi men use such facilities, nor indeed, that openly gay men do not, but to recognise that in these contested public spaces one's economic standing and English language proficiency do not hold much sway, and one's ulterior motive for visiting these sites is not so open to disclosure.

Gay gentrification

In contrast to the most marginalised sections of the gay population in Tower Hamlets, I now turn to some of the most settled and affluent sections of that population. James Polchin (1997) has argued that if it was the rise of industrial capitalism that created the opportunity for men and women to live independently outside of traditional family structures and experience or explore their homosexual erotic desires, then it has been the rise of consumerism and the connected belief that an individual can define his or herself through the goods and services they buy that has played a significant role in the development of gay 'communities' in the urban landscape. Aside from commercial venues, the most visible impact that gay men have had on the urban landscape is through the development of gay residential areas, which have often been created as part of the wider gentrification process.

In many ways, the phenomenon of specifically gay gentrification cannot

Queer spaces of Tower Hamlets

be seen as distinct from the broader process of gentrification, as middle-class gay men look for many of the same perceived advantages in a neighbourhood as other young professionals. Attracted by a relatively central location, the existence of relatively cheap housing, and the prospect of making a profit in the property market, gentrification has often taken place in those marginalised areas of the inner city (industrial areas, red-light districts or neighbourhoods with significant immigrant concentrations) where gay commercial venues have been located since before the partial decriminalisation of homosexuality in the late 1960s. However, in London, as in other cities, gay men (and women) have not participated uniformly in the gentrification process, but have concentrated themselves in a narrower range of neighbourhoods. In this section I shall explore a range of economic, geographical and cultural phenomena that have made Tower Hamlets an attractive location for gay gentrification.

The process of gentrification has been linked by a number of writers to capitalist crisis (Beauregard 1986; Harvey 1989; Smith 1986) claiming that the falling rate of profit from manufacturing and production, and the overproduction of commodities has led capital to seek new investment opportunities in other sectors, leading to a shift from production to investment in the built environment. In this situation, the most profitable opportunities have been found in those areas with a gap between capitalised and potential ground rent or saleable value. It is, however, important to see this process as part of the totality of social relations including the shift in the structure of the labour force towards service provision, administration and professional sectors; changes in family structure, related to the increased participation of women in the labour force and the related postponement of marriage and childbearing; and the growth of conspicuous consumption as a prime leisure activity.

In this process capital is quite prepared to seek out previously marginalised sections of society in an attempt to find new and more profitable forms of investment. Recently a number of mainstream businesses have developed an interest in the 'pink pound' as a means to exploit a section of society that is perceived to have a greater disposable income than the population at large. This trend can be witnessed in a number of spheres, from the large scale investment in gay pubs by the Bass Taverns brewery chain to the corporate sponsorship of the annual Lesbian, Gay, Bisexual and Transgendered Pride event by companies as diverse as United Airlines and Oddbins the wine merchants; but this process can be seen most clearly through gay gentrification and the targeting of some new property developments directly at the gay market by Bellway Homes and other property companies.

EMPLOYMENT OPPORTUNITIES

I believe that the nature of the local labour market in Tower Hamlets has contributed to making the area an attractive residential location for gay men. The borough's three largest employers are all relatively 'gay-friendly' public sector organisations: Tower Hamlets Council, the Royal Hospitals NHS Trust and Queen Mary & Westfield College. There is also a growing cluster of creative and cultural industries in the borough which, we may assume, have a significant gay cohort amongst their combined workforces.

In an American context, Larry Knopp (1992) has argued that the proportional decline in manufacturing employment and the concomitant rise in city centre service sector and administrative jobs has acted as a draw to the inner cities for first and second generation 'out' gay people, as these sectors have traditionally attracted a disproportionate number of gay people. While there is certainly more than a kernel of truth to this argument, it does imply that gay people do not find employment in other sectors, which is clearly not the case. It would be more accurate to say that these are areas of employment in which gay people are more likely to find an atmosphere in which they feel able to be open about their sexuality at work (at least in major urban centres).

HOUSING CHOICES

Warde (1991; quoted in Butler 1997, p. 43) has argued that while gentrification should be understood as the convergence of a number of different processes, these find expression in two significant forms: gentrification by capital and gentrification by (groups of) individuals through their social action. Both forms of gentrification have taken place in Tower Hamlets. The luxury warehouse conversions and other new developments that line the north bank of the Thames through Wapping, Limehouse and onto the Isle of Dogs are a prime example of gentrification by large capital. While gentrification by capital has mostly (but not exclusively) taken place in the south of the borough, gentrification by individuals' social action is a more obvious phenomenon in the north of Tower Hamlets, where several waves of young professionals have moved into the Victorian tenement blocks of Bethnal Green and the townhouses and terraces of Bow and Stepney, which mostly date from the same period.

Gay gentrification is more likely to take the form of gentrification by social action as individuals move to areas they associate (either recreationally or politically) with the gay scene in search of support, solidarity and safety, as well as the host of other social and economic advantages inner city areas hold for young professionals. It is perhaps not surprising, therefore, that it is my perception (and this has been reinforced by anecdotal evidence collected from a number of sources) that the gay population in Tower Hamlets is more concentrated in the north of the borough. Paul Barlow offers a further explanation as to why the area may have initially met the needs of those who became the first wave of gay gentrifiers:

> The main focus [of gay gentrification] has been in Bethnal Green. ... It's quite interesting really, Albert Jacobs used to be the leader of Bethnal Green Council and he had this policy that they were trying not to do too much slum clearance and they were trying to keep as many of the existing buildings; also there were a lot of charity buildings; and it wasn't as bombed as the rest of the borough. So as a result, there were a lot of fairly desirable small properties: single bedroom, two bedroom properties and they were also privatised quite early on which [made it easy for gay people to settle] there and in the latter part of the 1980s a lot of that stuff became very expensive, and there was that prestige of owning somewhere expensive as well.

So, for the first generation of gay gentrifiers in the area, and in recent years (since the bubble of the late 1980s property boom has burst) for newer first-time buyers, these small flats in old turn of the century tenement blocks have proved particularly attractive. For the slightly older, more monied, gay gentrifiers the borough has also offered a substantial stock of luxury apartments in converted warehouses and factories. The Bow Quarter development located in the former Bryant & May match factory, which is reputedly 40% gay (and rising, as its reputation spreads) is a prime example. Interestingly, at the time of writing, there are no gay commercial venues in the immediate vicinity of the Bow Quarter development, suggesting that gay men have chosen to live there for reasons other than the availability of a local commercial scene and that they have the economic capacity to lead their social lives on a London-wide scale.

In some respects, gay men are even more suited to gentrification of the 'loft-living' variety than other young professionals, as they require fewer rooms than heterosexual couples (as they do not generally need to make provision for children). And, for many gay people, it is the desirability and physical security of a property that is important, not whether it is located in a 'nice area'. Indeed, there is an implicit heterosexism in the notion of what constitutes a 'nice area'. The pull of the inner cities for gay people should not just be seen in the context of the social and economic advantages of these neighbourhoods, but also in terms of the negative aspects of suburbia. For many gay men it is far preferable to live amongst the diversity of an inner city area than the often stifling uniformity and conformism of a suburban district designed for the apocryphal nuclear family, which can impose unwelcomed attention on those who do lead alternative lifestyles.

COMMUNITY SAFETY

There is a general assumption that people choose to live in a place where they feel safe; but this is never a straight forward assessment: a concentrated, visible gay population can contribute to a collective feeling of safety, but visibility itself can act as a catalyst for attack. One of the first acts of the Tower Hamlets Lesbian and Gay Equalities Forum was to call a meeting on homophobic violence in the borough. This is an issue that has been taken up by the Tower Hamlets Lesbian and Gay Police Liaison Group, whose work is described below by Shahidul Miah of the council's Equalities Unit,

> [O]n it are representatives from both police divisions in the borough, the health authority and the council. It worked very well at the beginning - the first year and a half, I think, were very successful. We had Superintendent Wildman from Whitechapel Division (so we had it right from the top) present at the meetings, and Councillor Hinvest was also a regular attender. ... Whitechapel Division are very good. A lot of the initiatives that have come out of this have basically come out of Whitechapel. Limehouse has been a lot slower to respond.

While the tardiness of the police's Limehouse Division to respond to the issue of hate crimes against the borough's queer population is officially explained as the result of staffing problems, I question whether the issue is a higher priority for Whitechapel division given the apparent concentration of the gay male population in the north-west of the borough. On the issue of levels of homophobic violence in the borough, Shahidul Miah continues:

> But surprisingly, well not surprisingly, I'm glad that it is a relatively low number of incidents that are reported. On one level, that's good news, on another level, well, we need to look at whether there's a lot that's going unreported.

In the seven months from April 1997, twenty-eight incidents where an anti-gay motive was suspected were reported to the police in Tower Hamlets, most of them in the Bethnal Green and Whitechapel area. This figure is very similar to the number of incidents reported over the same period in Brixton, which also has a visible gay population.

Given that the figures for anti-gay hate crimes are not widely publicised, it is questionable to what extent the issue of community safety has influenced gay men to move to the area; although, the experience of living relatively free from harassment may be a deciding factor in encouraging men already resident in the area to stay. The issue of safety, however, is criss-crossed with contradictions as, for some men, the idea of living in what they perceive to be a rough and potentially dangerous working class district may have its own appeal.

URBAN AUTHENTICITY

It has been suggested that there is a connection between the gentrification of inner city areas and a search for 'urban authenticity' as witnessed in the stark interior design of so many loft apartments on both sides of the Atlantic (Serlin 1996); and a further connection for gay gentrifiers between this search for authenticity and the urban gay male body - particularly as expressed through the leather and skinhead subcultures, but also in a more general gay style that David Serlin describes as being 'based on an idealised version of gritty, urban rawness that supposedly invokes a pre-AIDS utopia of street sexuality.' It is interesting to note, in the context of this argument, that several of the gay commercial venues in Tower Hamlets either directly cater for the gay macho scene, or tolerate sex on premises in what one venue describes in its advertising as an 'interactive games room'. It is perhaps this yearning for urban authenticity, as much as the class divisions already discussed that has led a section of the local gay population to tolerate the shabbiness of so many bars in the area.

In his work on the evolution of the gay skinhead, Murray Healy (1996) has described how from the 1950s onwards youth subcultures allowed young working-class men to explore their sexuality in a homosocial environment far removed from the more 'nelly', cultured realm of the period's gay scene. In contrast to mods and hippies, Healy argues that the skinhead emphasised an (ultimately illusionary) 'authentic' working-class masculinity, and coincidentally developed at much the same time as the masculinisation of gay culture following the birth of the modern gay liberation movement. Ironically, between the decline of the original skinhead craze and its revival in the late 1970s, Healy suggests that it was largely gay skins who kept the image alive, allowing men space to adopt an image that signified their sexuality to other gay men, whilst not being read as such by the population at large, for whom the skinhead was still equated with street-fighting 'bovver boys'.

Both the first and second waves of the skinhead subculture found a base amongst working class youth in the East End, but amongst gay men the style has now been adopted by men of all social classes and is much in evidence amongst the (white) gay population in Tower Hamlets. Given the strong links between second wave skinheadism and neo-fascist groups, as well as the on-going history of vicious racist attacks against members of the Bangladeshi population in Tower Hamlets, the adoption of the skinhead style by some gay gentrifiers is telling. Although skinheads were not explicitly linked to the far right until the subculture's revival in the late 1970s, racist violence by skinheads was reported in the press from 1970 onwards. The skinhead emerged at the time when women, blacks and gays were harnessing their exclusion from mainstream society in order to identify themselves in radical opposition to the dominant culture. By contrast, the skinhead was an attempt to reclaim a dominant place in society for the white heterosexual male through a reliance on nostalgic notions of authentic working-class male sexuality that was ultimately conservative. While it is undeniable that there are a small number of black and Asian men who have adopted the skinhead style, this is does not negate the overwhelming whiteness of the image: ' [i]f 'If the frisson of eroticism conveyed by these styles depends on their connotations of masculine power then this concerns the kind of power traditionally associated with *white* masculinity' (Julien and Mercer 1987 quoted in Healy 1996: 144). Murray Healy sees a connection between this broader adoption of the style and both the fetishisation of working-class youth and the search for urban authenticity.

> Although signifiers of class can be adopted or changed, biographical facts are beyond the limits of self-reinvention. As the phrase in the *Boyz* feature [on the gay skinhead] 'genuine East End boyz' suggests, geography comes to displace class as a deciding factor in criteria of authentic skinhead status, because it has biographical implications. So if you cannot choose the conditions of your upbringing, you can at least choose where you want to live. (Healy, 1996 132)

If gay gentrification is seen as the spatial expression of identity construction and social activism against oppression, then it has to be asked to what extent it has become a deeply conservative phenomenon that has served to further marginalise queer people who are not white affluent men?

Regeneration: opportunities and dangers

If the continuing regeneration of the East End is not to further marginalise sections of the local population, strategies must be found that attempt to improve the quality of life for the majority, even if specific projects are focused on the needs of a particular section of society. One danger inherent in the project of regenerating East London is that short-termism and insufficient identification of investment assets and opportunities may lead the whole process to achieve little more that than 'jobless regeneration' created by gentrification (Clark 1997), which will not advance social justice for the majority of people living in the area. In this final section, by way of a conclusion, I shall briefly survey a number of ways in which the sizeable gay presence in Tower Hamlets can further contribute to the regeneration of the area.

EQUALITIES ISSUES

The Tower Hamlets's Equalities Unit is engaged in a number of important projects, some of which could potentially impact on the regeneration of the area. Of these, the Community Safety Initiative would seem to have the greatest potential for making a positive contribution to the quality of life for the largest number of people, gay and straight. However, if this project is to develop further, then a renewed and on-going process of consultation with the local queer population will need to be initiated in order to identify the extent to which anti-gay hate crimes *do* go unreported and to address any material problems that are highlighted by this research.

It is more than a little surprising, given the council's usual care in addressing the needs of the area's Bangladeshi population, that no work has yet been undertaken to identify the needs and aspirations of homosexually-orientated people from this and other ethnic minority communities. It seems worth considering whether, if the regeneration project is successful in raising the educational and economic standing of a greater proportion of the borough's population, this will create the conditions in which a larger number of South Asian queers are able to adopt a more openly 'gay' lifestyle, albeit one that retains a distinctively Asian perspective; what hybridised identities will arise and what effect this will have on the rest of the local queer population?

LEISURE AND TOURISM

Despite the closure of the London Apprentice, a mainstay of the London macho scene for many years, the cluster of gay venues in the Shoreditch area appears to be going from strength to strength. This small area has the advantage of being largely non-residential and so is well placed to support the night-time economy. However, there is the danger that if this area were to take off and be marketed as the East End's 'gay village' its development could strike a death knell to many of the smaller pubs in the rest of the borough, several of which would already appear to be struggling financially. As has been highlighted already, a number of these pubs currently cater for a slightly older, working-class gay clientele, who might otherwise not feel comfortable in, or be able to afford to frequent, more chic and trendy bars in Central London.

Here the example of Manchester's 'gay village' should serve as a cautionary tale (Hindle 1994; Quilley 1997; Whittle 1994). Manchester City Council and various gay entrepreneurs have hyped and marketed the gay village as part of the regeneration and reimaging of the post-industrial city centre, but this has created a situation where straight tourists now swamp the area hoping voyeuristically to sample the 'gay experience' for an evening. This calls into question just how 'safe' (and to an extent, how gay) the area still is; and has led to the increasing economic exclusion of large sections of the city's gay population, including many of those employed in low wage sectors of the area's service economy.

Gay men have certainly contributed much to making Tower Hamlets the area it is today, and this contribution goes far beyond their involvement in the gentrification process. As one of the broader strategies that is being considered for the continuing regeneration of London's East End is the greater promotion of the area's heritage and the development of tourism, it would seem sensible to identify ways in which the history and contemporary presence of gay people in the borough can be utilised to this end. The proposed 'Rich Mix' heritage centre planned for a site adjacent to Old Spitalfields Market might provide a starting point for this work. Given the success and popularity of both Madam Jo Jo's cabaret bar in Soho and Blackpool's Funny Girls bar, there might be some mileage in capitalising on the East End drag tradition, in much the same way as the Brick Lane Music hall has 'recreated' that particular brand of entertainment. There might also be sufficient scope for acknowledging the history of the area's gay presence through a series of pink memorial plaques, such as those erected by the REPOhistory Collective in lower Manhattan in the mid-1990s (Hertz, Eisenberg and Knauer, 1997), and linked to form an organised queer heritage trail. I am sure that with a bit more thought and a hint of camp wit some further imaginative ideas will come to the fore.

REFERENCES

Beauregard, R. (1986) 'The Chaos and Complexity of Gentrification' in Smith, N. and Williams, P. (eds.), *Gentrification of the City*, Boston: Allen & Unwin.

Bell, D. and Valentine, G. (eds.) (1995) *Mapping Desire: geographies of sexualities*, London: Routledge.

Binnie, J. (1996) 'Coming Out of Geography: towards a queer epistemology?' in *Environment and Planning D: Society and Space*, 15, 223-237.

Bouthillette, A. (1997) 'Queer and Gendered Housing: A Tale of Two Neighbourhoods in Vancouver' in Ingram, G. B., A. Bouthillette and Y. Retter (eds.), *Queers in Space: Communities/Public Places/Sites of Resistance*, Seattle: Bay Press.

Boyz, Issue 334, 6 December 1997, London: Chronos Publishing Ltd.

Butler, T. (1996) '"People like us": the gentrification of Hackney in the 1980s', in T. Butler and M. Rustin (eds.) *Rising in the East?: the regeneration of East London*, London: Lawrence & Wishart.

Butler, T. (1997) *Gentrification and the Middle Classes*, Aldershot, England: Ashgate Publishing Ltd.

Castells, M. and K. Murphy (1982) 'Cultural Identity and Urban Structure: The Spatial Organization of San Francisco's Gay Community' in Fainstein, N. I. and Fainstein, S. S. (eds.) *Urban Policy Under Capitalism*, London: Sage Publications.

Clark, G. (1997) 'Regenerating East London: where's the toolkit?' in *Rising East* Volume1, Number 2 : 55-72.

Cohen, P. (1996) 'All White on the Night? Narratives of nativism on the Isle of Dogs', in T. Butler and M. Rustin (eds.) *Rising in the East: the regeneration of East London*, London: Lawrence & Wishart.

Elder, G. S., L. Knopp and M. Brown, 'Review Symposium: George Chauncey's *Gay New York*' in *Environment and Planning D: Society and Space* 14: 755-70.

Gluckman, A. and B. Reed (eds.) (1997) *Homo Economics*, London: Routledge.

Harvey, D. (1973) *Social Justice and the City*, London: Edward Arnold.

Harvey, D. (1989) *The Condition of Postmodernity*, Oxford: Basil Blackwell.

Healy, M. (1996) *Gay Skins: Class, Masculinity and Queer Appropriation*, London: Cassell.

Hertz, B., E. Eisenberg and L.M. Knauer (1997) 'Queer Spaces in New York City: Places of Struggle/Places of Strength' in G.B. Ingram, A. Bouthillette and Y. Retter (eds.) *Queers in Space: Communities/Public Places/Sites of Resistance*, Seattle: Bay Press.

Hindle, P. (1994) 'Gay Communities and Gay Space in the City' in Whittle, S. (ed.) *The Margins of the City - Gay Men's Urban Lives*, Aldershot, England: Ashgate Publishing Ltd.

Hollister, J. (1997) *Lollipop Heaven: a highway rest area as a socially-reproducible site*; (http://sociology.adm.binghampton.edu/pages/hollister/LH1.txt).

Ingram, G. B., A. Bouthillette and Y. Retter (eds.) (1997) *Queers in Space: Communities/Public Places/Sites of Resistance*, Seattle: Bay Press.

Jay, E. (1997) 'Domestic Dykes: The Politics of "In-difference"' in G.B. Ingram, A. Bouthillette and Y. Retter (eds.) *Queers in Space: Communities/Public Places/Sites of Resistance*, Seattle: Bay Press.

Johnston, L. and G. Valentine (1995) 'Wherever I Lay My Girlfriend, That's My Home: The Performance and Surveillance of Lesbian Identities in Domestic Environments' in D. Bell and G. Valentine (eds.) *Mapping Desire: geographies of sexualities*, London: Routledge.

Keith, M. and S. Pile (eds.) (1993) *Place and the Politics of Identity*, London: Routledge.

Khan, S. (1991) *Khush, a report on the needs of South Asian lesbian and gay men in the UK*, Shakti.

Knopp, L. (1992) 'Sexuality and the spatial dynamics of capitalism' in *Environment and Planning D: Society and Space* 10: 651-69.

Mason, A. and A. Palmer (1996) *Queer Bashing: A national survey of hate crimes against lesbians and gay men*, London: Stonewall.

Mort, F. (1995) 'Archeologies of city life: commercial culture, masculinity and spatial relations in 1980s London' in *Environment and Planning D: Society and Space* 13: 573-90.

Norton, R. (1992) *Mother Clap's Molly House: the gay subculture in England 1700-1830*, London: Gay Men's Press.

Personal Interview; Paul Barlow, November 1997.

Personal Interview; Shahidul Miah, November 1997.

Polchin, J. (1997) 'Having Something to Wear: The Landscape of Identity on Christopher Street' in Ingram, G. B., A. Bouthillette and Y. Retter (eds.) *Queers in Space: Communities/Public Places/Sites of Resistance*, Seattle: Bay Press.

Power, L. (1995), *No Bath But Plenty of Bubbles: an oral history of the Gay Liberation Front 1970-73*, London: Cassell.

Quilley, S. (1997) 'Constructing Manchester's "New Urban Village": Gay Space in the Entrepreneurial City' in Ingram, G. B., A. Bouthillette and Y. Retter (eds.) *Queers in Space: Communities/Public Places/Sites of Resistance*, Seattle: Bay Press.

Serlin, D. (1996) *Gays, Ghettos, and the Politics of Urban Space in NYC*, draft of a paper later presented to the American Historical Association, January 1997.

Smith, N. (1986) 'Gentrification, the Frontier, and the Restructuring of Urban Space' in Smith, N. and P. Williams *Gentrification of the City*, Boston: Allen & Unwin.

Smith, N (1996) *The New Urban Frontier - Gentrification and the Revanchist City*, London: Routledge.

Smith, N. and P. Williams (1986) *Gentrification of the City*, Boston: Allen & Unwin.

Whittle, S. (1994) 'Consuming Differences: The Collaboration of the Gay Body with the Cultural State' in Whittle, S. (ed.) *The Margins of the City - Gay Men's Urban Lives*, Aldershot, England: Ashgate Publishing Ltd.

Whittle, S. (ed.) (1994) *The Margins of the City - Gay Men's Urban Lives*, Aldershot, England: Ashgate Publishing Ltd.

Widgery, D. (1993) *Some Lives: A GP's East End*, London: Simon & Schuster.

Interview With Michael Keith

Phil Cohen

Michael Keith is leader of Tower Hamlets Council as well as director of the Centre for Urban and Community Studies at Goldsmith's. In the interview with *Phil Cohen*, who is Director of the *Centre for New Ethnicities Research at the University of East London*, he talks about the thinking behind the Rich Mix Centre in Tower Hamlets, the concept of the Thames Gateway and also the Government's proposals for the governance of London.

Phil Cohen: Can we start with the Rich Mix Centre? I would like you to say a bit about the development of the idea, the politics, and its actual realisation.

Michael Keith: On one level the idea is so nebulous that it's quite easy to be vague about these things until the moment the project becomes specific and local; on the other hand there's something very local that's driving the whole project. The nebulous idea is obviously around cultural hybridity: the idea that new identities emerging in places like the East End are not built from ossified forms of ethnic essentialism, but are instead about different ways in which novelty appears, and what that means in terms of somewhere like East London as the entry point for generation after generation of migrants. Part of the agenda that flows from that is straightforwardly political. Effectively it will be a more politically progressive version of 'the people of London', an image which refigures London as always cosmopolitan in the past and increasingly cosmopolitan in the future. Migration is not new, what is seemingly familiar is actually quite strange in terms of where it comes from. If you like, to show the foreign inside the domestic, and also the ways in which the domestic itself is increasingly complex and involves people from different cultures and different parts of the world.

That broad idea around cultural hybridity is one that had a lot of backing and a lot of political capital in the late 1980s and early 1990s, when even people in the City were beginning to get worried about the rising tide of the far right in Europe and what that meant, and the agendas for a particular kind of tolerance that would work against the far right. It received a great impetus around the time of the success of Derek Beackon and the BNP on the Isle of Dogs.

But I think more pressing in terms of the local agenda is the question of what you do as a local government in late twentieth century Britain, when you have a large chunk of your community defined as one of the poorest in Britain; alongside the City, an ostentatious mark of affluence and a growing force in the area in terms of property values. You have a situation where there is a wall between the City and what surrounds it, which everyone agrees has existed for some time. Some people would argue that it has had negative effects, and some would argue that it has had positive effects.

There is this great fear, particular from the late 1980s onwards, of a steady eastward march of the City in property terms, particularly around the development of Spitalfields Market site, but also other key sites, for example, the old Bishopsgate goods yard, which is a massive area, and so there's both fear of office development moving eastward, but also fear of residential gentrification serving that office population.

In the face of that, a Banglatown campaign grew up locally, which was partly about trying to valorise what was there already as a centre of Bengali ethnicity. I think in terms of the local dimension of the Rich Mix Centre, part and parcel of the agenda, certainly from where I've been sitting wearing a political hat, which is Chair of Economic Development for two years, and now Leader, is that you cannot divorce, in any sense at all, the whole background of the Rich Mix Centre from what is happening in the west of the borough.

Phil Cohen: There seems potentially to be a tension between the kinds of ideas that are coming out in terms of Banglatown and what it represents politically, and the Rich Mix concept.

Michael Keith: One being backward looking and the other being forward looking? It's interesting how many people know what's coming out of Banglatown in terms of ideas, because it's like a kind of stone in the pond, all these ripples of rumours and gossip, and it gets down to the edge of the pond, and you find out all these things that are categorically, definitely coming out of Banglatown turn out to bear only a ripple-like resemblance to anything that's actually happened or is possibly going to happen in the future.

I think for Banglatown to work economically you need to make sure that there are enough attractions in that part of the City fringe to resist the change of land use from what is there now to office development and residential development. You can use planning laws helpfully to do that, but you also have to create some kind of viable economic base, and what that means is having tourist attractions and places where people can spend money.

Where people spend money at the moment is the restaurant trade, and the heart of Banglatown is Brick Lane, considered the centre of the restaurant trade, the catering trade. Symbolically, politically, sentimentally, in all sorts of other ways, Brick Lane means much more than just a load of restaurants, there's the relationship between the rag trade and the restaurant trade, the niche market and different retail bits and pieces, these are all deeply significant at all those levels. Put crudely, people are going to come in there to spend their money on Bengali food. Within the Banglatown idea you have gorgeous Hawksmoor churches, all within reach, one smack in the middle of that area and others within walking distance, you have the Jewish Heritage Centre, you have the Kobi Nazal Dance Centre, all of which are important buildings which are potentially being redeveloped as sites for people to come and visit.

None of those latter three are essentially Bengali, but they're all encompassed within the Banglatown notion. Banglatown has always been, from its roots as a protest movement against the extension of the City eastwards, an umbrella under which a wide range of interests shelter. The notion of Banglatown as about some kind of culturally essentialist celebration of Bengali ethnicity is, I think, a mistake. It doesn't mean that lots of people won't push it to mean that, but then these things are always contested. Lots of people will push for it and lots of people will push against it.

Phil Cohen: Some people might say - if you take Spitalfields - by putting the Rich Mix Centre in there, that what you're really doing is adding a little multicultual colour to an area to make it more attractive to the office workers and the tourists, it's just multi cultural colour. It's perhaps a criticism of flagship projects and cultural industries more generally, that the actual economic benefits to local communities, particularly from tourism, are not as great as they've been cracked up to be.

Michael Keith: I'm sure that's substantially right. There are two levels on which the question has to be answered. The first one is the rhetorical one: there is a kind of line which is totally nihilistic, which relates to the complete failure to rethink urban development. In particular, local economic development doesn't have a leftist impulse, beyond a few advocates of popular planning who take up that debate. But I think there will be a line that sees all forms of economic development as inevitably negative in their impact. That position becomes impossible to sustain when you've got major pressures of land use. So that's about pragmatic politics.

The second cut of the debate is how do you see this thing working eventually? What have you got there right now? You have an economic base - if you actually look at that area there are three bits to the economic base: the rag trade, the retail trade and the catering trade, all of which provide, to a greater or lesser extent, an employment base for the Bengali community.

Not exclusively, but those are the three chief sources of Bengali employment.

Potentially, the worst case scenario is that you get the eastward shift of the City. Some of those key sites: Bishopsgate, Spitalfields Market, one or two others, becoming the site of these big office developments, with kitsch boutique-type retail developing around there, driving up property values with massive increase in the residential market, since there's still quite a substantial private sector rental market which is vulnerable to gentrification. Then what you could have is the steamroller driving out of the Bengali community from that part of town. That is the worst case scenario and over a ten to fifteen years period.

If you're going to try to put together a plan that salvages something out of those trends, you have to base it on three lynch-pins: the retail trade, the rag trade and the catering trade. At the moment, the catering trade is down-market: people are coming to Brick Lane to eat pretty cheap food, and what is interesting - and this is a nation-wide phenomenon - what you see round here is a very rapid rise in more up-market curry houses. That has some interesting micro sociological dimensions to it, about who the food is for and who is able to eat it. You can still say, if you are talking about employment, the Banglatown debate sometimes polarises between the richer Bengali caterers, who are actually reinvesting in new, much more up-market, restaurants in Brick Lane, and some of the smaller people who are afraid of being squeezed out, because they are basically tenants. If landlords are aware of what's been happening in property development, the tenants, who are working at the cheap end of the restaurant trade, are in danger of being squeezed out all together.

That is a microcosm of all sorts of issues around the local plays of race and class. On a more mundane level, in terms of how you actually save the area, Banglatown is one of the ways you get an umbrella for the long-term future of the catering trade. For people to be spending their time and money there, either you have to pull in the kids that are out in the City on a Friday night or you've got to try and think about bringing more people in. What brings them in? The markets; Petticoat Lane, Brick Lane, Columbia Road, there is a chain of Sunday markets, there is also the specialist retail. Tens of thousands of people come into the market still, and that has got to be a way to draw people in.

But in addition you need other kinds of tourist attraction. These aren't necessarily what prompts people to spend their money, but then they often spend their money in the surrounding area. The other key tourist attractions within that framework are the Whitechapel Art Gallery, which has got a major expansion plan that the local council has been trying to work on, which would

Interview with Michael Keith

also potentially redevelop that Aldgate roundabout site, which is a nightmare. You've got the Rich Mix Centre, the Hawksmoor churches, and the prospective demand for the Jewish Heritage Centre, hopefully in the medium-term future. All of these will draw people in their own right, and then they'll go from there to spend their money later. The general idea is that there are millions and millions of people visiting the Tower of London who at present do not venture into the hinterland. There are ideas about having rickshaw rides from the Tower of London. I'm not totally sure about the plausibility.

Phil Cohen: Do you really want to go down that road? There is a marketing of Brick Lane and Whitechapel that reinforces the Gothic horror stereotype of the area as Jack-the-Ripper-land.

Michael Keith: You've already got these Jack the Ripper tour guys that flock round the area at night and I think that's far more offensive, it brings far less benefit to people than if they come down here, stroll around, voyeuristically stick their nose up against the curry house windows, and then bugger off back to the West End to spend their money there. That happens, and in a sense what we want is people to come down here and spend their budget here.

All the paradoxes of the tourist industry are well explored and well documented in terms of what that means. Whether you can commodify your own culture, sell it without selling your soul simultaneously, is a moot point. If you take Banglatown as an umbrella rather than as a kind of commodified essence, then I think that's one step in the right direction.

Having said that, yes, you are effectively commodifying Bengali culture, which if it works, you might find is exactly what people do when they're flogging their labour at sweated rates in the rag trade. It's always a very specific racialised identity that would be commodified there rather than within the labour market. So exactly how much can you commodify culture as opposed to commodifying other parts of manual labour - one is more or less oppressive than the other.

Phil Cohen: There is a specific mode of cultural labour that's involved here, so that raises an interesting argument: the difference between cultural capital and cultural labour is perhaps one of the emergent sites of debate, and possibly also of conflict.

Michael Keith: The racialisation of the rag trade is quite interesting in this context, in the sense of how those migrant networks keep feeding into this post-fordist labour boom of the mid-1980s. You get these specs drawn up, and these bog-standard clothes that are then produced elsewhere in the world, brought up to London and then customised here, just in time, for whatever the fashion styles are here. So you get things ripped off the Paris fashion walks, put on a computer screen, and someone gets a phone call: 'Can you do these in -'. This is what's happening in New York, Los Angeles, Paris, and in that sense the racialisation is not coincidental. The fact is that Polly Peck International was run by Turkish Cypriots, the connections then crossed over from the Turkish market into the Middle East. Fifty yards from where we are there are two leather factories both run by Pakistanis employing Bengali labour.

The Labour Party

Phil Cohen: Can I ask you for your thoughts about a viable strategy of economic regeneration for East London and the role of the council in that.

Michael Keith: I think part of that response, the most significant part of it, is a displacement of disillusion with the State. Obviously there are left and right articulations of it, but the notion that politically progressive projects can be carried out by central government or by the local state has taken all sorts of massive beatings that we all know about in a clichéd sort of way. But one is always interested in the left articulations to that, which I think are a mixture of the naive and the disingenuous. They presuppose some pure political world beyond the boundaries of the local state, and that comes back to an essentialised notion of civil society. Nor are we going to create this pure residue of community which is a territory of political virtue.

I think it's also the case that because of the events of the last twenty years there has been a dismembering of the traditional apparatuses by which both local and central government operate. I don't think that was all to the ill; most of the critiques of local government that were used by Thatcher or that came from the left in the early and mid 1970s, pretty well established the received cliché of the undemocratic nature of the local state, the dodgily representative or misrepresentative nature of the local state, and the forms of intolerance that were sanctioned by the local state. All of these produced a massive crisis of legitimacy for local government.

I don't think for a second that crisis of legitimacy has in any sense disappeared. It feeds into a situation where in the late 1990s you have probably an increasingly small, but vocal group of people who live on the romanticised story that all the powers of local government have been confiscated over the last 25 years; the time is now ripe to return them to the local government to recreate these halcyon days of the past, which is clearly nonsense.

But you also have people who say 'We're now living in this new world of stakeholding where there is a recognition of different stakeholders, among which representatives of local government, of local democracy, are players, but players among many other players'. I don't think that is necessarily altogether good or bad, but I do think that that argument has contingent properties which harbour both reactionaries and progressives.

There is a reactionary line, which effectively creates a spitting image world where everybody meets everyone else and you have 'luvvies' of local government, a new corporatism, where all the players are seen as equivalents. That equivalence basically destroys politics, because it is one thing to say that you have various private corporations with particular interests, you have various institutions of the public sector who have particular interests, you have various bits and pieces of governmental apparatus, and that government, or in trendy terms, governance, is a more complex thing than just a local authority. It is one thing to say that there is that complexity there on the ground, it is another thing to say that when you're deciding how to spend x amount of pounds through a particular line, then each of those organisations should have an equal stake in saying how that money should be spent.

Likewise, in terms of some of the more populist forms of communitarianism, you have this notion that there is a world beyond the state. There is a literature, particularly coming out of the collapse of the centrist left in Eastern Europe, proposing a reinvention of civil society as an arena of new political action. Communitarianism is one articulation of that, it's not the only one by any means, there are all sorts of versions of these celebrations of civil society that talk about political mobilisation beyond the state as being the political mobilisation that is effective, powerful and virtuous.

I think that's flawed, because it assumes that there is some straightforward boundary between what is the state and what is not the state. What is paradoxical about it is that the whole point, where the stakeholders's rhetoric comes from, is an acknowledgement that there are no simple boundaries between state and civil society. Michel Foucault talks about the boundary between state and civil society being a transactional boundary rather than a fixed one; that is precisely the point, when you actually begin to tease away some of these community groups that are these supposed residues of civic virtue, they're normally very well networked, particularly into networks that trace directly into the local state! I think the search for this pure territory of civil society is always going to be a chimeric search, because it can never be found.

Phil Cohen: I wondered how you saw the Labour Party?

Michael Keith: There are many things I dislike about the Labour Party, but one of the things I increasingly admire - a bizarre thing to say in these times - about the traditions of the Labour Party, is that effectively it is completely unprincipled, or it is based on the notion that you make your history but not in circumstances of your own choosing. If you accept that the boundary between regimes of governmentality, or between local government and what is not local government, is always going to be a a fuzzy boundary, then I think the party, in the political sense of the term, provides a vehicle by which part of that fuzzy boundary can be defined in a progressive sense.

The Labour Party provides a vehicle which is closer to any other mainstream agency by which a politically progressive culture can be achieved. I don't think one has to be naive or disingenuous about all the things the Labour Party stands for, all the things it has done or not done. I don't think it is a question of entryism or non-entryism, it's a question of saying if you're going to try and get something done you need to control local government and central government. Pragmatically, in order to do that, you need to work within a structure that has some populist resonance, and the answer to that is you work within the Labour Party. That constrains certain things but it also facilitates other things; it would be daft to pretend away either the constraints or the facilitation.

The Thames Gateway

Phil Cohen: The notion of the Thames Gateway seems to be a bandwagon, or a construct that people have got behind, and certain people seem to think this is the way forward, the idea of a sub-regional identity to attract inward investment, to deal with the spatial flows in the global city, and all of that. And the Thames Gateway is the name that is given to that kind of strategy and engagement. Other people are more sceptical and think it's window-dressing and conceals the fact that there are considerable problems about how different local authorities are going to get their act together and combine into coalitions of interest around particular projects. How do you see the Thames Gateway concept?

Michael Keith: Very crudely, I think there's a problem of matching the scale of problems to the scale of solutions. I don't mean geographical scale. There are various cuts of this again, cynically you could say the whole thing is a figment of Peter Hall's imagination, that Western London is overheated, overdeveloped, Eastern London is the opposite. It is something no more - or no less - complex than that. It has a certain power, there is a reality to the decline in manufacturing in Eastern London, there is a reality to big development sites in East London.

Interview with Michael Keith

However, that does not necessarily mean that key forms of economic development have a locus to them which makes commensurable sense at the same geographical scale. You then move into the political dimensions of it: you have a host of local authorities, very little money, and an ambiguous relationship to other definitions of the sub-region. For instance, there's a Lee Valley partnership subregion which crosses and in part overlaps with the Thames Gateway subregion. Both of those subregions have a legitimacy at a certain level of analysis; neither of them have that much money, although the Lee Valley region does have the virtue of being directly co-terminous with an Objective Two status European region.

When you start getting down to the nitty-gritty of the scale at which you match your solutions to your problems, I think what you have is vast swathes of poverty and underdeveloped land and development opportunites in the East of London, crossing a wide range of local authorities. The Docklands solution came out of the New Town ethos, it was bizarre and Thatcherite in its origin, but the Urban Development Corporations were a re-invention of some of the old New Town development corporations, the ideas behind both were that certain forms of local democratic operation didn't sit well with getting things done.

The New Town development corporations and the other development corporations were matched with vast resources to do things. Whatever one thinks of their successes or failures, they were financially backed. I'm not defending local authorities or local government for themselves in any sense, though there is a difficulty as soon as you sit on more than one local authority, it may be difficult to sit on one local authority in one place.

Phil Cohen: The idea of cross-river partnership seems to be difficult enough.

Michael Keith: It's logarithmic in its increase in problems. But that doesn't mean that the solutions will be easily forthcoming, unless you're going to back them with dosh.

The Future of London Green Paper

Phil Cohen: Finally: the government for London?

Michael Keith: What's interesting about the government for London is that it's almost the logical end-point of some of the more surreal debates about stakeholding; you can create so many stakeholders in this new corporatist world that you suddenly realise that none of them are very good at talking to each other, so by default you end up by reinventing the local government you abolished. There's almost a trans-political way in which that has been done. It doesn't have necessarily a right- or left-wing logic to it.

What I would fear, in a local government for London, is a model that effectively accepts the legitimacy of all the stake holders that are there, and then binds them into some contractual agency with some quasi-market government for London buying-in all the stakeholders that have been playing the game so badly for the last 15 years. What I would hope for is a rationalisation of many of those organisations being put together in a new structure.

Phil Cohen: What are your ideas about a Mayor of London and a London assembly?

Michael Keith: I am not as opposed to a mayor as many people are, but I think a logical position on that only makes sense within a sympathetic understanding of the role of the party system.

There's a politics of personality that has been foregrounded but which is always going to be there. The reality is that in 3 or 4 years' time we will probably see, by default as much as design, these fairly entrenched apparatuses of party machines getting their way, whether they select charismatic individuals or the products of those party machines. It will be interesting to see.

We are grateful to New Ethnicities *for giving us permission to reproduce this interview here; a version of the same interview will appear in a forthcoming issue of the newsletter.*

Interview with Michael Keith

Welfare to Work:

The East London dimension

Darren Simmonds

In this article *Darren Simmonds* explains the details of the Government's
Welfare to Work scheme and looks at how it will impact on the unemployed in
East London; he identifies a number of possible problems that will be
encountered in trying to get such an ambitious scheme off the ground so
quickly. In particular he asks whether it will reach those who are in most need of
training and whether it will really create new sustainable jobs.

Welfare to Work is not only a massive intervention on the part of the
Government into the labour market, it is also a rich vein of new titles, acronyms
and phrases. Before embarking on the discussion of what the programme
intends to achieve, the issues around this and the scale of the task I would
like to introduce some of the terms briefly.

- *Welfare to Work* (WtW): the umbrella name under which a number of
  new government interventions in the economy and labour market can
  be found.
- *The New Deals*: Young People (NDYP), Long Term Unemployed
  (NDLTU), Disabled and Lone Parents are each to be tackled under
  their own New Deal banner programme.
- *Unit of delivery*: the all-important geographic building blocks that are
  the basis for new partnerships and delivery plans for the New Deal for
  Young People and the New Deal for Long Term Unemployed.
- *Windfall Levy*: the tax levied on privatised public utilities on the excess
  profits they have generated since privatisation.
- *The Gateway*: the entry point to the New Deal provision. With
  counselling, careers advice, job search and basic skills provision.
- *Environmental Task Force* (ETF): one of the four options available to
  participants on the New Deal for Young People

- *Voluntary Sector Option* (VSO): another of the four choices open to young people based on participation of voluntary sector employers.
- *National Minimum Wage* (NMW): to be introduced within the lifetime of this government and most likely to affect the same people as being targeted under the Welfare to Work umbrella.
- *Employability*: not a concept born from the Welfare to Work but a key principal. The minimum set of personal and inter personal skills that enables a person to function to at least the lowest requirement of employers.

This article addresses the subject from three perspectives: firstly it seeks to explain the known content of the Welfare to Work programme; secondly the potential client group in the Thames Gateway region is analysed and thirdly some key issues and implications are assessed.

The Welfare to Work programme

Welfare to Work is one of the flagship projects upon which Labour based their manifesto and election campaign. It is also being billed as the largest labour market intervention for years, it is certainly the largest commitment of public funds for a single time limited training programme ever. The intention is to help those people who are currently dependent upon welfare payments to access employment opportunities. In order to do this the twin problems of benefit dependency and lack of minimum levels of employability must be addressed.

Employability is not a clearly defined concept, the values and abilities required by employers will vary. Rather than have a single set of defined employability skills the needs of the individual will need to be set against their expectations and capabilities and those of the employer. Nevertheless employability skills generally encompass;

- communication;
- the ability to work with others;
- literacy;
- numeracy; and
- the discipline of work.

Against the backdrop of making unemployed and excluded people more ready for employment it is also recognised that the current welfare system reduces the marginal benefit of employment for a number of current benefit recipients.

Given the bold statements of intent and the public consciousness of the scale of the project, what are the prospects for its success? The public awareness of Welfare to Work began long before the detail had been put in place. For many their first exposure would no doubt have been the budget announcement of the Windfall Levy on utilities to raise the £4.5bn estimated cost of the programme. Even from the first announcements it became clear a great deal of emphasis would be placed on the New Deal for young people with £3.15bn being earmarked for this alone. Following the budget announcement Welfare to Work and the New Deals have seldom been far from the headlines, many voices have been heard as the issues have been raised and a great diversity of groups have entered the discussions over the shape Welfare to Work would take. Consequently hopes are high in a number of quarters for a programme that is not yet fully defined.

Briefly I will explain the labour market and benefit system interventions planned under the Welfare to Work umbrella.

MINIMUM WAGE AND BENEFIT REFORM

Outside of the New Deals work has already started on the implementation of a National Minimum Wage (NMW). The Low Pay Commission (LPC) is an independent advisory body set up to recommend to the Prime Minister the initial level at which a National Minimum Wage might be set in the United Kingdom. Allied to this will be the work carried out on benefit tapers; the underlying intention is to reduce the marginal rate of taxation for people re-entering the workforce and as far as possible remove the problems associated with the 'benefits trap'. While the NMW, which could be set somewhere around £3.50, or perhaps £3.75, will not affect the majority of full-time employees in London, those most disadvantaged in the jobs market are more likely to be affected. People working part-time, many of whom are women and those entering or re-entering employment at the lowest occupational levels and rates of pay run the are those more likely to be affected.

THE NEW DEAL FOR LONE PARENTS

The New Deal for lone parents will focus on those parents whose youngest child is already of school age. These parents will receive help and advice from the local Job Centre and with the assistance of an individual advisor an action plan covering training, job search activity and after school childcare will be drawn up. The Government has stressed that this will be a voluntary service, this has not however stopped concerns being raised over possible compulsion, coercion and enforcement. The Government has also recognised the importance of flexible childcare provision for school aged children if this strategy is to work. To this end the 'childcare disregard', the earned income ignored when calculating eligibility to benefit payments will be raised to £100 per week for two or more children and be available for consideration on children up to 12 years of age. The disregard currently stands at £60 and only applies to children up to the age of 11. Lottery monies will also be made available for the development of out of school childcare clubs. In total the Government believes around 1,000,000 lone parents are dependent upon benefit across the country and that around half of these have a youngest child already of school age. In London as a whole these figures translate to a total of just under 200,000 lone parents in receipt of benefit, with possibly half of them eligible under this part of the Welfare to Work programme. As part of an exercise to measure the interest this programme could generate once it goes live, the Employment Service has assessed demand to be around 10-15 per cent of those people eligible. This part of Welfare to Work will be organised on a regional basis with some provision being made available to parents who have just become eligible as of April 1998. The stock of parents with children already of school age will have to wait until October 1998 before the programme is fully operational.

THE NEW DEAL FOR PEOPLE WITH A DISABILITY OR LONG TERM SICKNESS

In order to assist people with health problems or disabilities back into employment the government has earmarked £200m from the windfall levy. The intention is to test a range of options aimed at improving access to employment 'in partnership' with the people, representative bodies, employers, government departments and local authorities. Separate from this New Deal a review of benefits payment to people with disabilities is also underway. Similarly to the New Deal for Lone Parents administration of this part of Welfare to Work is liable to be regionally based.

NEW DEAL FOR THE LONG TERM UNEMPLOYED

This part of the New Deal initially was to concentrate solely on those people aged over 25 who have been unemployed for more than two years. Recently however this client group has been increased to include, initially on a pilot basis, people unemployed between 12 and 18 months and between 18 months and two years. For a long while the single confirmed element of this New Deal was the offer of £75 a week subsidy for up to 26 weeks to employers recruiting from this client group with additional training support. It had also been stated that there would be opportunities to study for up to twelve months to reach an accredited qualification. At the same time as announcing the extension to the client group Employment Minister Andrew Smith also announced that the Gateway provision available to the younger New Deal clients would be extended to this client group as well. Given the staggered implementation of the New Deals and the relative monetary values assigned to the budgets it is not surprising that the development of this New Deal for Long Term Unemployed has taken something of a back seat to that for the younger unemployed.

NEW DEAL FOR THE YOUNG UNEMPLOYED

So far it has been the New Deal for young people that has captured most attention, while awareness of the concept of Welfare to Work and this New Deal has been high the understanding of the details have not always been as high or easy to assess.

Secretary of State for Education and Employment David Blunkett announcing the launch of the New Deal for Young People on 3 July 1997 said,

> The programme is based on three principles: quality, continuity and employability. By combining these three we will offer a long-term prospect to both those taking part in the programme and those helping us to deliver it. Quality will be built in at each stage, whilst employability will be an essential feature recognised in the education and training programmes which are critical to all four options.' (*Source:* DfEE press release 3 July 1997.)

All of these principals are easy to accept as fundamental requirements. The NDYP must be seen as a qualitative and not a quantitative programme, while there will no doubt be some element of target-setting the key to success will not be how many people have entered the process but what benefit they gain from the programme. The emphasis on continuity is a recognition that the New Deal is setting out to achieve a single particular aim, it is also intended that the New Deal be a one-off programme for the lifetime of this parliament. If this is to be realistic the New Deal can only be seen as one part of the move towards to embedding the lifelong learning culture in these young people. It is also acknowledgement that New Deal will not be the entire solution for many of these people, but merely a way of starting them in the right direction. The third principal that of employability is the main aim of this New Deal, without these skills these young people can never effectively compete in the labour market.

Unlike the previous administration the development of the New Deal for Young People has been an open process. Rather than develop a central model of the New Deal that was then rolled out from the DfEE, the decision was taken to allow local flexibility down to the level of plans being written by local partnerships. The New Deal as well as offering employability skills to those most at need has also created a new geographic map of England and introduced the term 'Unit of Delivery'.

With the decision of the Government to task the Employment Service with responsibility for delivery of the New Deal a new set of official boundaries achieved a state of importance they had never seen before. By tasking Employment Service District managers with delivery plan development and responsibility for delivery of the programme the boundaries they were working to have become the basis for new strategic and operational partnerships. It is fair to say the administrative boundaries within the Employment Service have been largely determined by volume of traffic and are not based on travel to work patterns or directly related to economic activity. The 17 Districts in London do not conform easily to any other administrative boundary. As one single example the City of Westminster forms part of three separate Employment Service Districts. The first task facing the parties interested in helping the Employment Service was to establish new partnerships capable of delivering the New Deal. Although the Employment Service has lead responsibility for the New Deal it was acknowledged that this was not a feat they could achieve in isolation. It would take a robust and active partnership of local strategic bodies to assist the process. Even within organisations such as TEC's and local authorities with a history of partnership development based on the need for collaboration over issues such as challenge funding this was not an easy task.

The period of consultation allowed every interested group a chance to be involved in the development of the New Deal for young people. The range of people consulted included TEC's, local authorities, careers services, employers, probation service, community organisations, voluntary organisations, colleges, Members of Parliament, Chambers of Commerce and training providers, to name but a few.

At the time of conception the figure of 250,000 young people nationally was being presented as the size of the task and the political target. In the subsequent months two factors have been acknowledged that affect this thinking fundamentally. Firstly, the overall numbers of unemployed have dropped so dramatically that the stock of young people aged between 18 and 24 and unemployed over 6 months in the entire United Kingdom stood at only 122,096 in October 1997. Secondly, while the stock of unemployed is the most obvious and visible reference to assess the size of the client group, the flows, into and out off the client group, are also essential. The assessment of how many young people may need the assistance being offered, across a given time period cannot be completed without stock and flow information. As the numbers of young people unemployed has fallen the onus has changed from the quantity driven provision of assistance for 250,000 people, to a quality driven desire to make a real difference to those people still unemployed with no headline target figure. It is interesting to note that had the overall stock of young people unemployed over 6 months remained at roughly the 250,000 figure the effects of people joining the group would result in a large amount of need remaining unanswered. While the reduction in unemployment is welcomed the challenge facing the New Deal is how to improve the employability of those people who even in this currently buoyant labour market cannot secure employment. With unemployment reaching its lowest point since 1989 the people currently left unemployed who have been so for some time are patently those with the least impressive job skills to offer employers or those least willing to take up employment.

The New Deal for young people offers staged provision of services aimed at improving the overall employability of the individual. A great emphasis will be placed on attempting to meet the needs of the individual. It is perfectly feasible, although challenging from the delivery viewpoint, to have every single person entering the programme receiving a unique personal service. First contact for the young person will be with the Employment Service via a client-facing member of staff; at this point the Gateway process will begin.

The Gateway must provide a range of services to fit the needs of each individual. The portfolio of provision available must be able to meet the needs of people from diverse groups, such as the homeless, people with health problems and disabilities, and those who need help with basic skills. The precise pattern of Gateway activity will depend on the individual's needs and circumstances. Certain elements will be provided, or available to all, others will be made available according to need. The Gateway is being described as 'an intensive period of counselling, advice and guidance' also 'each young person will have both an individual ES adviser and opportunities to take advantage of independent careers guidance. For example, those who need help to improve their basic skills will have the chance to do so before progressing into one of the New Deal's four options for young people.'

It is hoped that the Gateway will lead to a high number of young people finding employment outside of the New Deal framework. Nationally it is hoped that 40 per cent of the young people who pass the six month unemployment milestone and enter the New Deal will need no further assistance than that which they receive inside the Gateway. Given the complexity of the client group and the individual needs of clients it is acknowledged that no single organisation will have the range of skills to deal with a client group.

While the concept of delivering the New Deal from a single site Gateway has many attractions and benefits, this is unlikely to be the case. Provision may not be a single site activity in no short part because no single organisation will be providing it, while initial contact will be with the Employment Service specialist advice and guidance on careers will probably come from another organisation. As well as these two major players a number of specialised organisations such as the probation service will also play a part in the Gateway process. The volumes of people entering the Gateway, particularly in the first six months, will place a great strain of the space available to the Employment Service and their partners, the uneven nature of the demand in the first year however will also place a premium on available space. No funds are expected to be made available for capital or infrastructure development in order for organisations to be able to deliver any parts of New Deal.

People will enter the Gateway at their first 'Restart' interview after the programme goes live in April 1998. An unemployed person receives a Restart interview every six months, for those people unemployed less than six months this will be their first Restart interview, for others their first after April 1998. The decision to process both the entire stock and all the new inflow into the client group will lead to a peak in demand over the first six months that will not be matched in subsequent periods. This will be looked at in further detail later in this article.

The Gateway can last up to four months, only a very few clients will remain for this length of time, working assumptions have been made nationally as to how long people will remain in the Gateway. It is not expected that people will leave the Gateway to go on to one of the three employment-related options (see table below) within the first couple of months. Those people leaving to enter full-time education and training, however, are expected to be identified early and leave the Gateway within the first month. It is also hoped that many young people will be able to leave to unsubsidised employment in the first two months, following enhanced job search and some basic skills work. After this initial two-month period people are expected to

The East London dimension

start leaving to the subsidised employment option. After month three, those not yet able to secure employment will be encouraged to consider entry to the Voluntary and Environmental Task Force options. At the end of month four it will be necessary to make mandatory referrals into the four options for those people who had not so far secured a place. There is no recognised fifth option of remaining unemployed and receiving benefit.

DIRECTIONS FROM THE GATEWAY

Full-Time Education and Training With a maximum duration of 12 months, this is the longest of the four options available. The aim is to take those young people with the lowest levels of employability, expected to be those with least or no qualifications, and improve their skills and qualifications base so they can become competitive in the labour market.

Employment with Subsidy This option can last for up to 26 weeks and the employer concerned will receive a £60 a week subsidy for each young person. An additional £750 will also be available to pay for training towards a recognised qualification, this training must be the equivalent of one day a week and for the majority of young people this training will probably have to be delivered away from the usual place of work.

Environmental Task Force With a duration of up to 26 weeks this option will encourage young people to take part in community-based activities which have a beneficial effect upon the local environment. Again the equivalent of one day a week training to a recognised qualification will be provided and financed by the provision of £750. As a further incentive to the young person they will receive a benefits top up of £15.38 a week, a total of £400 over the 26 weeks.

Voluntary Sector Option Similarly to the Environmental Task Force this option will run for a maximum 26 weeks with the same training and extra benefit entitlement. The young people will be able to benefit from work experience within voluntary organisations while the organisation can benefit from additional resource at only minimum cost to them.

Each of the employment-related options offer one day a week (or equivalent) of training and development. It is important that this development is carefully planned and delivered. Quality training must be made available not just with respect to recognised qualifications but also to enable the young people to develop the non-accredited skills and attributes that are important to enhance employability. This broad-based training plan will require the involvement of a range of training suppliers with very different areas of specialism.

The training and development offered not just under the three employment related options but also the full time education and training will need to engage the young people and encourage participation. Given the client group and their history and perception of past schemes this training will need to offer value that the young people can openly recognise. The courses and qualifications undertaken need to offer real value together with new and innovative methods for reaching a client group that in many respects has a 'been there, seen it, done it' mentality.

Vital to the success of the New Deal is the breadth and quality of the opportunities made available to these young people. Employers will need to be found that not only offer the opportunity of employment for young people, but also the possibility of progression. Efforts must be made to differentiate this programme from other government-sponsored initiatives that these young people may have been exposed to in the past.

Even the non-direct employment options must offer something new that can be seen to enhance employability. To some the Environmental Task Force and Voluntary options will be seen as consolation prize, where greatest benefit will be derived by the organisation and not the individual. These projects must be able to demonstrate the benefit they offer to the individual in order to be considered acceptable within the New Deal framework.

Irrespective of the option taken by the young people there must be a sense of value to the provision they receive. Those unable to enter employment with a subsidy, which many will see as the best available option, must still value the training and experience they receive. Young people place great value in the opinions of their peers and the New Deal must appeal to this peer review group in order to be a success. A number of these young people will have been disaffected through school or a lack of success on other government-sponsored schemes.

The New Deal client groups are already the focus of mainstream training provision. Training for Work is the most obvious area of potential overlap but other TEC programmes, European Social Fund (ESF) schemes, Single Regeneration Budget (SRB) provision and much voluntary provision also seeks to improve the conditions faced by New Deal clients. It is conceivable that the organisations currently delivering these other programmes for young and unemployed people will also deliver some

The East London dimension

elements of the New Deals, it is important that synergy can be achieved between the New Deal and existing provision. As the New Deal is a time bound programme that does not purport to be the only solution for these excluded people, it is important that current provision be maintained as both an alternative to complement for the New Deals.

The New Deal in the Thames Gateway area

Having detailed the intended interventions planned under the New Deals the question remains who are these people and what kind of provision will be required to assist them?

Analysis into the actual composition of the client group will obviously not be possible until the programme goes live in April. The information presented here includes analysis of the current and recent unemployed that match the eligibility criteria. If the New Deal had gone live in October 1997 there would have been in excess of 25,000 clients within the 12 local authority districts of the Thames Gateway area. These clients are not just those that qualify automatically for the New Deal for Young People (NDYP) but also those that definitely qualify for the New Deal for the Long Term Unemployed (NDLTU). If the New Deal for Long Term Unemployed is extended after the pilot phase to include all those aged 25 and over and unemployed more than one year this total would rise to 35,000.

To qualify for this group individuals must be in receipt of Job Seekers Allowance and have been unemployed in excess of the minimum time period. These minimum periods are currently 26 weeks for those aged 18-24 and 104 weeks for those aged 25 and over, at the time of writing the extension of the New Deal for the Long Term Unemployed to include those unemployed for less time has not been confirmed. While it is acknowledged that the criteria for participation under the New Deal framework allows for early entry of certain groups this analysis concentrates on those people who have passed these duration thresholds.

THE CLIENT GROUP OF THE NEW DEAL FOR YOUNG PEOPLE

As would be expected the greater concentration of New Deal clients are to be found in the boroughs closest to the City of London which traditionally have high unemployment levels. The table below includes both the count of unemployed but also expresses this as a percentage of the Thames Gateway area as a whole.

Table 1: Young unemployed in the Thames Gateway

October 1997	18–24 unemployed 6 months plus	
Area	Number	percent
Barking & Dagenham	425	4.9
Bexley	405	4.7
Dartford	166	1.9
Greenwich	1,005	11.6
Hackney	1,444	16.7
Havering	275	3.2
Lewisham	1,095	12.6
Newham	1,224	14.1
Redbridge	489	5.6
Thurrock	318	3.7
Tower Hamlets	1,014	11.7
Waltham Forest	814	9.4
Totals	**8,674**	**100.0**

Source: NOMIS.

The largest concentration of NDYP clients can be found in Hackney, Newham, Lewisham, Tower Hamlets and Greenwich. Four out of these five boroughs are in the Skills for the Millennium SRB area, each of these boroughs as of October 1997 had more than one thousand young people eligible for the New Deal. Between them these five account for two-thirds of the total number of clients in the Thames Gateway area and if Waltham Forest is also included we find that half the boroughs contain over three-quarters of the young people eligible. At the other end of the scale Dartford, Havering and Thurrock each have less than 320 potential New Deal clients.

Comparing October 1997 with October 1996, the number of NDYP clients has fallen from 15,308 to 8,674. Representing a fall of 6,634 or 43 per cent. Levels of unemployment have been falling for some time since they reach their highest point in early 1993 and the total number of New Deal clients now stands at a similar level to those seen as we entered the 1990s. By the middle of next year there is every chance that the total number of people unemployed will have reached a new low point, even lower than that in 1989. In addition to the growth in jobs available and the underlying positive economic conditions, one other factor that will have contributed to these low

The East London dimension

unemployment figures is the introduction of the Job Seekers Allowance.

Concerns about the conflict between need and eligibility to JSA are not confined to the New Deals, by restricting access to the New Deals to JSA claimant only the possibility exists that some of those in greatest need may be further excluded from accessing employment. Outside of the New Deal framework consideration needs to be given to the people being excluded from the benefit system who are genuinely in needs of the assistance programmes like Welfare to Work are intended to provide.

As well as the stock of clients at any given point in time, it is also important to consider the people joining the client group as time passes. In the three months up to October 1997 2,478 people joined this young person client group. From October 1996 to October 1997 a total of 11,856 young people passed the six-month unemployment threshold. Over the 12 local authority districts this equates to 1,000 a month. The boroughs with the highest in flow activity are not unsurprisingly those with the highest stock totals. One area of caution when considering these inflow figures is the

Table 2: Inflows and outflows of young unemployed

Year from October 1996 to October 1997	18 –24 unemployed 6 months plus in flow and out flow	
Area	In flow	Outflow
Barking & Dagenham	642	992
Bexley	575	947
Dartford	231	365
Greenwich	1,247	1,857
Hackney	1,669	2,560
Havering	491	790
Lewisham	1,354	2,182
Newham	1,721	2,733
Redbridge	857	1,278
Thurrock	478	691
Tower Hamlets	1,467	2,221
Waltham Forest	1,124	1,874
Totals	**11,856**	**18,490**

Source: NOMIS.

possibility of double counting. Over the course of a complete year it would be possible for a young person to be considered as part of the New Deal client group twice. This could happen if a person eligible for New Deal at the start of the year, or becoming so soon after, left unemployment for a brief period and rejoined early enough to have been unemployed for six months by the end of the year.

The total number of young people who had been eligible for the year to October 1997 for the whole Thames Gateway region was 1.8 times the stock figure at the beginning of the year.

While it can be seen that across an entire year from October 1996, over 27,000 young people in the Thames Gateway area either were or became eligible for the New Deal for Young People, only 8,674 remained eligible at October 1997. In total a net 18,490 young people left the register during this time a figure 1.2 times greater than the number eligible at the beginning of the year and more than twice the residual stock at the end of the year. This natural movement of young people into and out of unemployment is currently occurring without the assistance of New Deal. Given that the level and type of support that is currently provided will continue to be available after the provision under New Deal commences the problem of dead weight begins to arise. The 19,000 young people who had been part of the potential client group during the year in question would appear at first sight to have found solutions without the need for any greater assistance than is currently being provided.

The flow of clients into the New Deal for Young People will not be consistent over the first year but should find a more consistent monthly flow in year two. The decision to have the New Deal begin at the first restart interview young people receive after the start of the programme, will result in the entire stock of long term unemployed as well as all those joining this group to be processed within the first six months. By October 1998 the only people entering the NDYP will be those people receiving their first restart interview as they reach six months plus unemployment.

In the three Employment Service districts covering the London East TEC area the expected flow of clients into the NDYP is displayed in the table below. The combination of these three Employment Service districts cover the six boroughs of Barking and Dagenham, Havering, Newham, Tower Hamlets, Redbridge and Waltham Forest, it also includes a small part of the local authority area of Epping Forest.

These client flow figures are taken from the Delivery Plans from each of these districts as they were presented to the regional assessment panels. As can be seen a great deal of variation is expected concerning the volume of

Table 3: Flow of NDYP clients into programme within LETEC area

Totals	In flow
April-98	1,407
May-98	1,031
June-98	1,090
July-98	1,275
August-98	1,064
September-98	938
October-98	517
November-98	668
December-98	907
January-99	904
February-99	944
March-99	711
Total	11,456

Source: Employment Service Delivery Plans.

The peak of demand can be seen more clearly on the graph below.

In flow NDYP within LETEC area

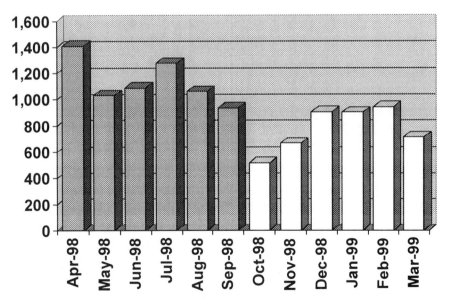

clients entering the programme. Part of the variety is down to the seasonal nature of unemployment even in an economy like London. Another element of the variation is the inclusion of all the stock of unemployed in the entrants during the first six months. In the first six months it is anticipated that 6,805 young people will enter the Gateway, this will then fall to 4,651 in the second 6 months. On a daily basis these figures represent an average peak of 74 clients per day in April and a average low point of 23 clients per day in October. The fact that demand for places in the Gateway, and subsequently the four options, will be 50 per cent higher in the first six months than the subsequent six months will have knock on effects not just upon the resources required from the Employment Service but also the providers of other services.

Analysis of the wider London labour market, however, shows that most of the young people leaving unemployment are not finding permanent solutions. Looking at data for the preceding year from the Labour Force Survey across London only around one in three of those leaving youth unemployment could have been absorbed by the growth in employment. Others will have found temporary solutions, some within employment others in training and education destinations.

From these two areas we can see that in terms of unemployment and employment the labour market with respect of young people is very dynamic. This will in no small part be due to the variety of options open to young people after compulsory education ends. This dynamic labour market however will have a great impact upon the demands placed on the New Deal. It would be impossible to remove from the New Deal provision those people who find alternative outcomes without the assistance on offer, what can be hoped for however is that with some additional advice and guidance, at this point of their personal development, some of the churning in and out of jobs and employment can be reduced.

Another issue to be addressed is that of substitution. The hope is that young people with advice guidance and some basic skills enhancement will secure employment, either directly or via one of the New Deal options. If young people do gain a competitive advantage in the labour market the question that will need addressing is who then becomes disadvantaged. Without economic growth and an overall increase in employment, people achieving positive outcomes from Welfare to Work will only achieve at the expense of others. The possibility exists that by presenting employers with the option of employing a young person with a subsidy payment may reduce the availability of jobs to young people who do not qualify for the New Deal. Beyond young people who have not been unemployed long enough, the older unemployed who are not part of the New Deal for Long Term

The East London dimension

Unemployed may also be equally disadvantaged, these include:

- non employed, non JSA claimants, labour market returnees etc;
- employees seeking to change jobs;
- people under 18 wishing to enter the labour market.

The client group as it stands in April 1998 will be an interesting mix of frictional unemployed and many young people with severe employability issues. Analysis of the Labour Force Survey on a pan London basis shows that a high number of clients will have poor educational achievements, an equally high number will have poor work records and significant number will have literacy and numeracy issues.

The Labour Force Survey while useful for analysis of the client group for the New Deal does have some drawbacks. The nature of surveys will always result in levels of accuracy not being guaranteed when small sub area of sub population analysis is undertaken. To ensure an acceptable level of accuracy Labour Force Survey data reported here is taken from the pan London level and from surveys over the period 1995/1996.

It is estimated that over 40 per cent of the client group will have no work history. Surveys carried out by the Employment Service support this figure but suggest that there are geographic variations. In the Employment Service districts covered by London East Training and Enterprise Council, the likelihood of having held a job prior to becoming unemployed was higher the further the claimant lived central London.

The fact that such a high percentage of young people have not worked before is in some part due to the age profile of the individuals concerned. With an increasing number of young people staying on past the statutory school leaving age and an increasing number delaying their entry into the labour market, this high level of joblessness will reflect that many of these people have only recently entered the labour market. The combination of people undertaking second and third activities post school and the ever increasing numbers passing through higher education will both be making a contribution to this level. Some element of this joblessness will be due to people seeking the right kind of employment for their perceived abilities post further and higher education.

While there are a higher percentage of graduates in London, both employed and unemployed, than nationally a high proportion of the unemployed have little or no educational achievement.

Analysis of the Labour Force survey carried out by the Policy Studies Institute has identified the approximate level of the highest qualification

Table 4: Qualifications of the young unemployed

Percentage with highest qualification at these NVQ levels

NVQ level	Qualification type	percent
NVQ 4 and above	HND, Degree and higher	12
NVQ 3	Mainly A level's	15
NVQ 2	Mainly GCSE grades A-C	34
NVQ 1 or 'Other qualifications'	GCSE grades below A-C	20
No qualifications		20

Source: PSI, LFS.

held by the young unemployed in London.

Whilst one in eight are educated to a degree level, around one in four of the young unemployed have either no qualifications or only very basic levels of qualifications.

For perhaps the first time in a high profile government-sponsored programme the issue of equality is very high on the agenda, as well as the specific New Deals for Lone Parent and people with a disability or long-term sickness equality of opportunity by ethnicity is also under consideration. Unemployment rates are higher amongst minority ethnic groups. The New Deal delivery plans acknowledge that as certain groups are increasingly disadvantaged in accessing employment action needs to be taken to improve individual competitiveness. In the Employment Service districts that cover the London East Training and Enterprise area around one in three New Deal clients will come from minority ethnic groups.

NEW DEAL FOR LONG TERM UNEMPLOYED

Whereas the total New Deal for Young People client group represents around one in ten of the total number of people unemployed, the New Deal for Long Term Unemployed, those unemployed over two years, are roughly twice the number and therefore represent just under one in five.

The boroughs with the highest numbers of Long Term Unemployed aged 25 and over are again Hackney, Lewisham, Greenwich, Tower Hamlets, Newham and Waltham Forest. These six boroughs account for 77 per cent of the total client group in the Thames Gateway area.

While Lewisham and Newham have broadly similar total numbers of people unemployed, the size of the NDLTU client group varies greatly

Table 5: Long term unemployed

October 1997 Area	25 years and older unemployed more than two years	
	Number	percent
Barking & Dagenham	677	4.1
Bexley	860	5.2
Dartford	340	2.1
Greenwich	2,084	12.6
Hackney	3,065	18.5
Havering	509	3.1
Lewisham	3,010	18.1
Newham	1,551	9.3
Redbridge	864	5.2
Thurrock	586	3.5
Tower Hamlets	1,665	10.0
Waltham Forest	1,398	8.4
Totals	16,609	100.0

Source: NOMIS.

between them; Lewisham has twice the number of NDLTU client of Newham.

In October 1996 the total number of people eligible for NDLTU in the twelve boroughs of the Thames Gateway was 28,251. By October 1997 this had fallen to 16,609, this fall of 11,642 is a decrease of 41 per cent and is comparable with the fall of 43 per cent seen by the young person client group. Both these decreases within the young person and long term unemployed groups exceed those seen by the unemployment total for the area. Across the twelve boroughs of the Thames Gateway region total unemployment fell by 28 per cent between October 1996 and October 1997.

As well as the confirmed targeting of those people unemployed over two years the piloting of the programme for people unemployed one year and 18 months opens the possibility of even greater levels of participation.

The initial pilots are likely to concentrate upon the younger elements eligible for the New Deal for Long Term Unemployed with people aged 25 to 35 currently being the most client group most discussed.

In addition to the client group described above the expansion of the NDLTU would have made an extra 9,671 people eligible in October 1997. Of these people over the age of 25 and unemployed between one and two years 4,229 are aged between 25 and 35. If the pilot eligibility criteria for NDLTU are extended to the main programme the total client group across the 12 Thames Gateway boroughs in October 1997 would have been 26,580. When this figure is added to those eligible for NDYP the total client group in October 1997 would have been 34,954 which represents just under 40 per cent of the total number of unemployed people in the 12 boroughs. On a borough by borough basis the relative percentages of all unemployed who would be considered eligible for the New Deal for Young People and Long Term Unemployed are detailed in the table below.

Should the New Deal's succeed uniformly across the twelve boroughs the greatest gains in absolute terms should be seen in Hackney, Lewisham and Greenwich. These three boroughs would also see the greatest reduction in the overall levels of their unemployment.

Table 6: Percentage of all unemployed eligible for The New Deals by area

October 1997	18-24 & unemployed	25 and older and unemployed			All Ages
	More than 6 months	Between 12-18 months	Between 18 months and 2 years	More than 2 years	Total New Deal Clients
Barking & Dagenham	10.0	5.3	4.8	15.9	36.0
Bexley	8.6	5.0	4.8	18.2	36.6
Dartford	8.9	6.0	4.3	18.2	37.3
Greenwich	10.7	6.3	4.6	22.3	43.9
Hackney	10.3	6.8	5.0	21.8	43.8
Havering	7.5	6.2	4.4	13.8	31.9
Lewisham	9.2	6.8	4.9	25.3	46.1
Newham	10.9	6.5	3.8	13.8	34.9
Redbridge	7.9	6.1	3.7	13.9	31.7
Thurrock	10.7	6.1	4.3	19.7	40.8
Tower Hamlets	10.5	6.7	4.5	17.2	38.8
Waltham Forest	9.5	7.0	4.3	16.3	37.1
Totals	9.8	6.4	4.5	18.7	39.5

Source: NOMIS.

Issues and implications

So far I have looked at the theory of the New Deals and Welfare to Work and the kind of people involved, the final question I intend to address is what needs to be done and what can we expect to happen? In short the practical outcomes and issues are based on the theory.

Firstly, a number of organisation need to adapt very quickly to the new provision called for to make the New Deals a success. As the accountable body the manner in which the Employment Service adapts is key to the ongoing success of the programme as is the speed at which service providers can not only match demand once the programme is live, but also react to the changing nature of this demand.

The second key outcome will need to be the rapid development of flexible and targeted advice guidance and training. This training will need to consider two main problems - the low or relatively low starting point of many of these clients and the fact that much of the New Deal client group will have negative experiences of government-sponsored initiatives either firsthand or via their peers. Much still needs to be done to remove the stigma of government schemes. The young people who are first to enter the programme will need to see the progression routes they have from their current position to that of employment.

A great deal of effort will undoubtedly need to be invested in ensuring the expectations of young people are realistic. One of the interesting aspects of some focus group work undertaken as part of the New Deal process is the expectation of young people in relation to jobs and earnings. As part of joint London TEC's response to the New Deal immediately after the general election a series of focus groups were held with young unemployed people from various inner London boroughs. The consensus of opinion was that young people had unrealistic expectations of their worth to employers and the kinds of work they would be asked to perform. Many of the young people taking part in the focus groups used their potential earning power from non-mainstream activities to benchmark their expectations. Some small part of these responses can be attributed to the nature of the young people's circumstances and the manner in which they view the jobs market. Activities such as petty thieving, the supplying of drugs or use of the benefit system are areas that these young people could easily see providing a ready return for little effort, a factor that influences their motivation to pursue full time employment. While the views of a small number of young people in central London will not necessarily match those of other young people up and down the country they do highlight the task faced by the New Deal programme in this area.

Consistency of delivery will be difficult to achieve given the manner in which partnerships have been developed. Across units of delivery strategic partnerships have each developed as unique bodies, initially delivery is therefore likely to be unique to each delivery area. The myriad of providers involved across the geographic spread of New Deal means that no two areas will be able to follow the sample model of provision. It will be interesting to see how viable it is for the large number of small providers to continue their provision after the initial influx of people into the New Deal programmes has slowed to the lower and more consistent demand expected in year two. From the start of proceedings the Government has made it clear that they do not expect the New Deal to be a profit-making exercise for the organisations involved. There is a question mark over the continued participation of organisations with either a profit motive or the need to generate surpluses to support other provision or infrastructure development. The Government are faced with the double standard of requiring organisations that receive funding from the public purse being asked not to take a profit from a programme that actively seeks the involvement of profit making private sector bodies.

The ultimate aim of the New Deals is to move people from welfare dependency to employment. This will not be possible without employers willing to recruit; both as part of the scheme and after people have left. To make just the New Deal employment options a success a large number of employers will need to be found who are willing to take on New Deal clients.

The LETEC Employer Survey of 1997 indicated employers were only vaguely aware of the details of the New Deals, 30 per cent stated they had 'not heard of the initiative' and only 6 per cent claimed to be 'fully aware of the details'. The degree to which employers might be interested varied significantly; opinion was split evenly with a roughly equal number of companies responding yes to each of the three possible answers 'would be interested', 'would not be interested' and 'maybe/unsure'. The reasoning behind the negative 'would not be interested' responses does not offer much hope of a change of heart on the part of employers even given a greater understanding of the programme. Of those companies responding 'would not be interested' the majority 52 per cent said it was for one of two reasons, either 'no suitable jobs for young people' or no jobs likely to be available in the near future'. Given this background a major challenge to the success of the New Deals will be finding the employment opportunities for New Deal clients to take up.

On the positive side regarding employer's involvement very few employers who would be interested stated that New Deal employees would be used to replace existing employees, 48 per cent of respondents suggested there would be 'new jobs or positions in the establishment', while 31 per cent thought new employees would fill 'existing unfilled positions'.

The New Deals are not expecting on their own to be the one stop wonder cure for all the problems faced by young people and the long-term unemployed in accessing employment. During the duration of the programme it will be impossible to achieve a 100 per cent success rate of people into jobs, what the New Deals will need to be able to demonstrate is the progression that a person can make using the New Deal as the start. To do this current provision and external support or indeed further programmes and support must fit seamlessly together with the New Deal to build upon the progress already made. The need to provide the correct exit strategy for people unable to secure employment as a direct result of the New Deals will go a long way in demonstrating a commitment to these disadvantaged people not seen before.

The New Deals are time-bound programmes and are intended to perform a one off reduction in the total number of people unemployed. It is important therefore that steps are taken to prevent future generation of people falling into the unemployment trap that so many of the New Deal clients seem unable to escape from without assistance. To achieve this all elements of training and education must be looked at with a view to providing the necessary employability skills within the training and education infrastructure currently available.

It is obviously too early in the lifetime of the Welfare to Work programme to make too many critical conclusions. It is difficult to be sure of the overall impact the programmes will have. The potential for great benefit exists, unfortunately there also exists a chance of failure. The profile of the programme and the level of funding earmarked for its delivery have raised expectations above that of previous government-sponsored initiatives. This high profile however can be seen as a double-edged sword, on one side the profile works as a great marshalling point for the enthusiastic and committed to rally around, it also means any level of failure will be magnified by the high hopes held. The programme is based on a genuine desire to meet a genuine need, the ability of the wide variety of bodies required to bring these changes about is critical to the success of the programme. No single part of Welfare to Work can succeed in isolation, increasing access to job opportunities for the unemployed will not help everybody without a review of the marginal rate of taxation. Assisting lone parent to seek employment cannot succeed without additional affordable childcare support to make it possible. Flexibility is the key term for success, this flexibility however will need to exist within a guiding framework. For accountability purposes there will no have to be advice, guidelines and rules concerning activities under Welfare to Work, what must be achieved is the retention of flexibility within these rules to really address client needs.

The New Deals will have to be able to process a very high number of clients in the lifetime of the programme and seek to achieve considerable results from the very start to demonstrate their value. In the first instance, however, the New Deals will not have the benefit of the other welfare reforms to aid their achievement and will have to rely upon the goodwill developed to see it through the inevitable teething problems. Welfare to Work does stand a considerable chance of success if patience and common sense are allowed to prevail over dogmatism and the need for a quick fix.

Demography, family diversity and changing household structures throughout London East

Vikki Rix

Over the past twenty-five years, a number of profound changes have been taking place within the composition of both families and households. Nationally, and across all European nations, rapid fertility decline, the ageing of the population, marital decline, rising divorce rates, remarriage, an increase in cohabitation and having children outside of marriage have led to a diversification of family forms and family lifestyles (Ditch *et al* 1996, Bradshaw 1996 Ruxton, 1996).

Households containing married couples with dependent children have become less common, whilst the growth of lone parent families and lone parent households has been substantial. Single person households have also become much more widespread, particularly amongst the elderly. Throughout the 1980s, the continuing growth of women's participation in the labour market has contributed to the rise of 'dual earner' households. At the same time, however, households without any adults working have also increased due to economic restructuring, labour market insecurity and high unemployment (Barclay 1995, Ditch *et al* 1995).

Children and families, therefore, have become major issues of sociological and political debate. Throughout Britain, family break down and the decline of 'traditional' family values have become increasingly associated with inner city decline, delinquency and the widespread educational failure of Britain's youth (Edwards and Duncan 1997, Millar 1996). The previous neo-conservative government and the 'back to basics' campaign placed lone parents, particularly lone mothers, at the forefront of this debate. There is no doubt that changing family and work patterns, along with ageing, have also placed heavy demands on Britain's welfare state; a welfare regime ill-equipped to cope with widespread demographic and socio-economic change. Since 1979, for example, the social security budget has risen from 23 per cent to 31 per cent in the UK (Harker 1996). Having reviewed some key national trends, the essential focus of this article is to explore the changing demography, family and household patterns of the London East sub region. Again this is rather timely and significant, considering New Labour's modernisation of Britain's welfare state and the national implementation of welfare to work later this year. The first section reviews the changing population of London East, outlining variations in the age and ethnic composition of local boroughs. Turning to family life and household composition, the second section examines the prevalence of traditional and new family forms throughout London East boroughs.[1] A comprehensive discussion on the rising number of lone parent family households is provided, examining the implications of welfare to work for both existing and new lone parents. The social geography of both 'work poor' and 'dual earner' households is compared, along with the London East increase

in single person households.

The Changing Demography

POPULATION TRENDS

Throughout the 1970s and 1980s, the population of London East, like London as a whole, continued to decline largely as a result of high rates of net out-migration (Rix 1996). Focusing on the 1980s, Hackney, Lewisham and Southwark were still losing residents at a faster rate than London as a whole. The loss of local residents, however, was especially high in the borough of Hackney. In 1981, for example, Hackney's population was 179,529. By 1991, this had dropped to 161,590, an overall population decline of 10 per cent.[2] Between 1981 and 1991, the rate of population decline similarly exceeded the London average of 4.9 per cent, and the Outer London average of 3.9 per cent in the outer London East districts of Greenwich, Waltham Forest, Barking and Dagenham and Havering. In comparison , the loss of local residents was far lower in the localities of Thurrock, Bexley, Dartford and Redbridge. By contrast, Tower Hamlets was the only London borough to experience an increase in population, rising from 139,996 in 1981 to 150,533 in 1991, an increase of 7.5 per cent. This divergence was entirely due to a high rate of natural change in that there were more births than deaths (Rix 1996).

More recently, however, all London East boroughs, like London as a whole, have recorded an increase in population. Natural change, net migration and various borough boundary changes have contributed to the reversal of population decline (Focus on London, 1997). In London as a whole, the local resident population had risen to around 7 million by 1995.[3] By contrast, the London East sub-region had around 2.5 million residents, a local population larger than most other major cities. For example, just over 1 million people lived in Birmingham compared to 0.6 million in Glasgow (Rustin 1997, Regional Trends 1997). Looking at local variations, the largest increase in population has taken place in the inner London East boroughs, particularly Hackney and Southwark. 1995 mid-year population estimates show that the local resident population of Hackney had risen to 194,000, whilst Southwark's local population had risen from 196,442 in 1991 to 232,000 in 1995. Table 1 shows that the outer London East boroughs of

Table 1   Population change in London East

1981 population base				1995 population
	Residents		1981-1991	Residents
London East	1981	1991	% change	1995
Thurrock	126,311	124,684	-1.3	132,000
Bexley	214,355	211,418	-1.4	220,000
Redbridge	224,731	219,925	-2.1	227,000
Dartford	80,250	77,573	-3.3	84,000
Newham	209,128	199,346	-4.7	228,000
Greenwich	209,873	198,199	-5.6	211,000
Waltham Forest	214,595	201,823	-5.9	221,000
Barking&Dagenham	148,979	140,039	-6.0	155,000
Southwark	209,735	196,442	-6.3	232,000
Havering	239,788	224,636	-6.3	231,000
Lewisham	230,488	213,595	-7.3	240,000
Tower Hamlets	139,996	150,533	7.5	173,000
Hackney	179,529	161,590	-10.0	194,000
Greater London	6,608,767	6,287,426	-4.9	7,007,000

Source: 1981 and 1991 Census, Crown Copyright; Regional Trends 1997.

Havering, Bexley and Redbridge recorded the smallest increase in the local resident population. In 1995, however, the majority of London East boroughs had over 200,000 local residents, whilst Dartford and Thurrock had a much smaller local population of 84,000 and 132,000 respectively.

London East's ethnic communities

London has always been a region of ethnic and cultural diversity (Storkey 1996). In the early 1990s, nearly half of all Britain's ethnic minority population of around 3 million lived within the Greater London region. Not surprisingly, around one and a half million residents living in London were born outside the UK, whilst a fifth classified themselves as non-white in 1991. As a result of continued immigration, around thirty-seven different communities have now settled within the London metropolis, a major cosmopolitan city, in which 180 different languages are spoken (Storkey 1996). The growing racial and cultural diversity of London is a particularly significant feature of inner London East's demography. Newham, for example, has one of the most racially and culturally diverse populations of all London boroughs. In 1991, just over two-fifths of the borough's population was non-white, double the London average of 20 per cent. The neighbouring localities of Hackney and Tower Hamlets also had

over a third of residents from ethnic groups other than white. South of the river, Lewisham and Southwark had a smaller ethnic minority population of 22 per cent and 24.4 per cent respectively. The geographical spread of different ethnic communities, however, highlights considerable diversity. In 1991, for example, nearly three-quarters of ethnic minority residents living in Lewisham and Southwark were either Black Caribbean, Black African or Black Other. This compared with nearly two-thirds in Hackney, far exceeding the London average of 39.8 per cent. By contrast, the neighbouring boroughs of Tower Hamlets and Newham had an exceptionally high proportion of non-white residents from the Indian, Pakistani and Bangladeshi communities.

Travelling eastwards, both north and south of the River Thames, the local resident population has remained predominantly white and British born. In 1991, for example, over 90 per cent of local residents living in Thurrock, Dartford, Bexley, Barking and Dagenham and Havering were white and UK born. Redbridge and Waltham Forest, however, were interesting exceptions. Bordering Hackney and Newham, over a quarter of residents were non-white in Waltham Forest compared to 21.4 per cent in Redbridge. Exploring the geographical settlement of various ethnic groups in outer London East highlights the widespread prevalence

Table 2   1991 ethnic composition, London East

London East	Percentage of local residents in ethnic groups other than white	Percentage of non-white residents who were			
		Black	Indian/Pakistani Bangladeshi	Chinese	Other
Thurrock	2.4	21.7	42.7	13.6	22.0
Havering	3.2	29.6	40.8	11.2	18.4
Dartford	4.0	15.5	49.5	8.5	26.5
Bexley	5.8	24.1	46.2	9.6	20.1
Barking&Dagenham	6.8	34.2	47.9	6.1	11.8
Greenwich	12.7	42.0	33.0	6.3	18.7
Redbridge	21.4	19.8	64.9	3.2	12.1
Lewisham	22.0	73.9	8.2	4.7	13.2
Southwark	24.4	72.7	10.4	5.2	11.7
Waltham Forest	25.6	44.1	41.0	2.3	12.6
Hackney	33.6	65.5	18.7	3.2	12.6
Tower Hamlets	35.6	19.9	69.4	3.2	7.5
Newham	42.3	33.9	53.8	1.9	10.4
Greater London	20.1	39.8	38.7	4.2	17.3
Inner London	25.6	52.4	27.1	4.4	16.1
Outer London	16.9	28.2	49.2	4.0	18.6

Source: 1991 Census, Crown Copyright.

of Indian, Pakistani and Bangladeshi residents. For example, nearly two-thirds of all ethnic minority residents were from those particular communities in Redbridge. By contrast, both Waltham Forest and Greenwich had a much higher proportion of Black residents. Interestingly, the Chinese community had a much greater presence in outer London East, particularly in the boroughs of Thurrock and Havering.

Recent projections obtained from the London Research Centre show how the ethnic minority population may have grown throughout London and London East since 1991. In London as a whole, projections show the non-white population growing from 20.1 per cent in 1991 to 23.4 per cent in 1996 (Storkey, Maguire and Lewis 1997). Focusing on London East localities, Newham's ethnic minority population may have risen to just over half in 1996, the highest of all London boroughs. In outer London East, the

London average 23.·

% residents		
3.90 -	8.90	☐
11.10 -	22.30	▤
24.70 -	50.00	■

Map 1: 1996 ethnic minority projections for London boroughs

non-white population may have risen to just over 30 per cent in Waltham Forest, and to just over a quarter in neighbouring Redbridge. Although 1996 population projections highlight a slight increase in ethnic minority groups in Havering, Bexley and Barking and Dagenham, those boroughs still had less than 10 per cent of non-white residents.[4] Mapping ethnic minority projections clearly shows the continued inner and outer London East polarisation.

FERTILITY PATTERNS AND AGE PROFILE

Over the past two decades, the declining number of children and the delaying of child bearing amongst women has been a fundamental shift in social behaviour. In the 1990s, women are certainly having far fewer children across all European industrialised nations (Bradshaw *et al* 1996). As a direct consequence, all European member states now have fertility rates below the required population replacement level (Ditch *et al* 1996). In Britain, for example, the average number of children per woman[5] has declined from 2.72 in 1960 to only 1.71 in the late 1990s[6] (Bradshaw 1996). Turning to London-wide trends, although female fertility rates have fluctuated throughout the 1980s and 1990s, the average number of children per woman has remained slightly higher than the national average. In 1983, London's female

Table 3 Changing fertility patterns of women living in London East

	Total Period Fertility Rates		
London East	1983	1991	1995
Havering	1.56	1.73	1.61
Bexley	1.64	1.83	1.72
Lewisham	1.71	1.75	1.75
Redbridge	1.71	1.84	1.82
Greenwich	1.85	2.01	1.89
Waltham Forest	1.95	2.00	1.90
Barking&Dagenham	1.76	2.05	1.94
Southwark	1.90	1.90	1.97
Hackney	2.10	2.20	2.07
Tower Hamlets	2.54	2.32	2.42
Newham	2.17	2.36	2.46
Greater London	1.71	1.76	1.73
UK	1.81	1.82	1.71

Source: Annual Abstract of Greater London Statistics, Regional Trends 1997.

fertility rate was 1.71. By 1991, this had slightly risen to 1.76, declining again to 1.73 in 1995.

Examining local patterns, women living in London East generally have high fertility rates. In 1995, for example, the average number of children per woman exceeded the national and London average of 1.71 and 1.73 in all London East boroughs, apart from Havering. London East variations, however, have persisted, clearly portraying the inner and outer London East divergence. Travelling eastwards out to the more suburban districts of Havering, Bexley, Dartford, Redbridge and Thurrock, local resident women tend to have fewer children.[7] In Havering and Bexley, for example, women had on average only 1.61 and 1.72 children in 1995, compared to over two children in Newham, Tower Hamlets and Hackney. In fact, both Newham and Tower Hamlets had the highest and second highest fertility rates of all London boroughs in 1995. Interestingly, Lewisham recorded a strikingly low female fertility rate of 1.75 when compared with neighbouring inner London East localities. With regards to outer

Graph 1 Changing proportion of children aged under five, London East

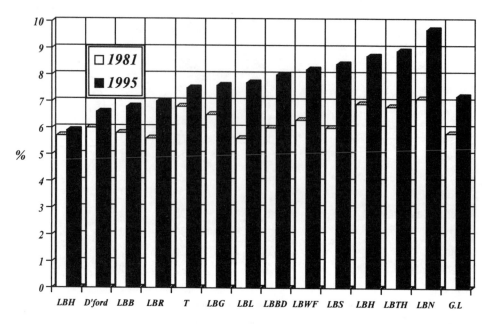

LBH=Havering, D'ford=Dartford, LBB=Bexley, LBR=Redbridge, T=Thurrock, LBG=Greenwich, LBL=Lewisham,
LBBD=Barking&Dagenham, LBWF=Waltham Forest, LBS=Southwark, LBH=Hackney, LBTH=Tower Hamlets,
LBN=Newham, G.L=Greater London

London East, Barking and Dagenham similarly diverged from surrounding neighbourhoods. On average women living within this locality had around two children in 1995, the second highest fertility rate of all Outer London districts and the sixth highest in London (*Regional Trends* 1997).[8]

Due to the high fertility rates of local women, all London East boroughs have experienced an increase in the proportion of children of pre-school age since the early 1980s. As a result, the proportion of under fives exceeded the London average of 7.2 per cent in all London East boroughs, apart from Bexley, Redbridge and Havering. The inner

London East borough of Newham had the highest proportion of children aged under five of all London boroughs, 9.7 per cent in 1995 compared with 7.1 per cent in 1981. Tower Hamlets, Hackney and Southwark, as well as Waltham Forest and Barking and Dagenham , also had over 8 per cent of children aged 0-4 in 1995, compared with around 6 per cent in the early 1980s. The proportion of under fives, however, has remained generally lower in other outer London East boroughs. Less than 6 per cent of children were aged 0-4 in Havering, the lowest of all Outer London boroughs. 1995 population estimates also illustrate the continued

134

presence of large numbers of school aged children living in our London East sub region. Again, all London East boroughs recorded an above London average proportion of children aged between five and fifteen. This was far more pronounced in Tower Hamlets and Newham, where nearly a fifth of children were of school age, the highest of all London boroughs and way above the London average of 13.3 per cent.

Examining other aspects of age also highlights significant features of London East's demography. In 1995, all London East boroughs had a below London average proportion of working age residents. In Barking and Dagenham and Tower Hamlets, for example, only 58 per cent and 59.9 per cent of residents were of working age compared to the London average of 64 per cent. By contrast, however, the proportion of residents of working age was above the respective Kent and Essex county averages of 60.4 per cent

Table 4 1995 age structure of London East boroughs

London East	Percentage of population aged		
	5-15	16 up to PA	PA&over
Dartford	13.3	63.6	16.5
Southwark	13.6	63.6	14.4
Havering	13.7	61.2	19.2
Lewisham	13.7	63.4	15.2
Waltham Forest	13.8	63.0	15.0
Bexley	14.0	61.7	17.5
Redbridge	14.0	61.9	17.1
Thurrock	14.5	62.9	15.2
Barking&Dagenham	15.0	58.0	19.0
Hackney	15.0	63.7	12.6
Greenwich	15.3	60.9	16.2
Newham	17.1	60.9	12.2
Tower Hamlets	17.3	59.9	13.9
London	13.3	64.0	15.5
Essex	13.7	61.1	18.7
Kent	14.1	60.4	19.0

PA=Pensionable age
Source: Regional Trends 1997.

and 61.1 per cent in Dartford and Thurrock (*Regional Trends* 1997). Given the lower rates of net out-migration, the elderly community has remained far more prevalent in outer London East boroughs. In 1995, only Greenwich, Redbridge, Bexley, Barking and Dagenham and Havering recorded an above London average proportion of elderly residents. This was particularly the case in Barking and Dagenham and Havering, which had nearly a fifth of residents of pensionable age and above. This compared with around 12 per cent and 14 per cent in inner London East localities, where ethnic diversity is contributing to the younger age profile.

The London East sub region, therefore, has quite a unique and diverse social demography. The ethnic minority population is much larger in inner London East boroughs, which is also home for large numbers of young children of both pre-school and school age. Fewer elderly residents, however, live in inner London East. By contrast, outer London East localities have remained overwhelmingly white and British born, although Waltham Forest and Redbridge were two exceptions. The proportion of young children is also high, particularly in Barking and Dagenham, Greenwich and Waltham Forest. The elderly community is much more widespread in outer London East. In the next section of this article, I shall explore the changing patterns of family life and household composition throughout the London East sub region.

Changing Family[9] Structures

MARITAL DECLINE AND DIVORCE

Since the early 1970s, the popularity of marriage, particularly amongst young people, has rapidly declined. The number of first time marriages, for example, has nearly halved in Britain, declining from around 400,000 in 1970 to only 201,000 in 1994. During the same period, the numbers divorcing have more than trebled (*Social Focus on Families* 1997). In 1990's Britain, nine per cent of all marriages ended in divorce within two years compared with only one per cent in 1961. Drawing on the 1981 and 1991 Censuses, both marital decline and divorce have similarly permeated London and London East. Among younger residents, aged between sixteen and twenty-nine, there was a shift away from marriage in all London and London East boroughs. This was largely as a result of the increased propensity of remaining single. Focusing on London East, between 1981 and 1991, marital decline amongst residents aged 16-29 was particularly high in Thurrock, Waltham Forest and Newham. For example, the proportion of young people married in Thurrock dropped from over 40 per cent to just under 30 per cent, and from just over a third to less than a quarter in Waltham Forest. In Newham, whereas 38 per cent of young residents were married in 1981, ten years later this had dropped to around a quarter. Despite the general trend of marital decline, however, young people living in London East were still more likely to be married compared with young people in London as a whole. In 1991, only Southwark, Hackney and Lewisham diverged from this marital pattern, having nearly 80 per cent of young single residents.

Between 1981 and 1991, marital decline also occurred in the older age groups in all London East boroughs, primarily due to divorce, as well as an increased likelihood of remaining single. This was particularly pronounced in Hackney, Lewisham and Southwark, where the proportion of residents married between the ages of 30 to retirement declined by 15 per cent and 14 per cent respectively. This decline far exceeded the London average rate of marital decline of nine per cent. Not surprisingly, those inner London East localities had an exceptionally high proportion of older residents remaining single. Hackney, for example, had 30.1 per cent of residents of working age still single in 1991, compared to less than 10 per cent in Bexley and Havering. Table 5 (overleaf) shows that marital decline was far less common for residents of working age in outer London East, although Greenwich and Waltham Forest were interesting exceptions.

Exploring patterns of marriage and divorce clearly shows the interweaving of both old and new traditions in our London East sub region. In 1991, for example, all London East boroughs recorded an above London average proportion of both young people married and divorced. Only Waltham Forest and Redbridge diverged from the pattern of divorce. Amongst those residents of working age, divorce was far more common in Hackney, Southwark, Lewisham and Tower Hamlets, as well as Greenwich and Barking and Dagenham. In fact, the impact of old and new family lifestyles is perhaps particularly striking in the relatively homogenous locality of Barking and Dagenham. In 1991, this particular borough had both the highest proportion of young people married and divorced of all London boroughs. Whereas 29 per cent of young people were married, around three per cent were also divorced, nearly twice the London average of one-and-a-half per cent.

MARRIED COUPLE FAMILIES

As a consequence of marital decline and rising divorce rates, married couple families with dependent children have become far less widespread throughout Britain. In 1986, for example, nearly half of all families were married couples with dependent children. By 1994, this had further declined to 42 per cent (Haskey 1996). Throughout the same period,

Table 5 Marital decline

	1991 16-29	81-91	1991 30-64/ 59	81-91
London East	% M	%change	% M	%change
Southwark	18.4	-10.0	57.4	-14.0
Lewisham	18.9	-9.0	61.7	-14.0
Hackney	19.2	-7.0	54.5	-15.0
Waltham Forest	22.2	-13.0	68.8	-11.0
Redbridge	22.7	-9.0	76.5	-6.0
Greenwich	22.8	-12.0	70.0	-10.0
Tower Hamlets	22.8	-9.0	61.9	-10.0
Havering	22.9	-11.0	81.2	-6.0
Newham	25.7	-12.0	68.9	-9.0
Bexley	26.1	-10.0	79.8	-6.0
Dartford	27.9	-10.0	75.0	-5.0
Barking&Dagenham	29.1	-10.0	73.4	-8.0
Thurrock	29.3	-14.0	74.7	-7.0
London	20.1	-9.0	67.7	-9.0
Inner London	17.3	-8.0	57.2	-11.0
Outer London	22.1	-10.0	73.8	-10.0

M=Married

Source: 1981 and 1991 Census, Crown Copyright.

however, 'new' family forms, such as cohabiting families and lone parent families, continued to rise. Nationally, for example, cohabiting couple families doubled from five per cent to 11 per cent between 1986 and 1994, whilst lone parent families rose from 12 per cent to nearly a fifth (Haskey 1986, *Social Focus on Families,* 1997). In relation to family composition,

geographical variations have remained highly significant. Married couple families with dependent children, for example, are more widespread in central, rural counties of England, whilst new family forms are more prevalent in urban areas like London (Haskey 1996).

Unfortunately, the lack of comparative local data restricts the

138

investigation of London East trends. Although the 1991 Census constructed a variety of family types (Dale and Marsh 1993), 1981 comparative data is not available. Drawing on the 1991 Census family indicators,[10] therefore, shows that married couple families were far more numerous in the traditional stable localities of outer London East. In Dartford, Havering and Bexley, over a third of all families comprised of married couples without any children, all above the London average of 30.4 per cent. In fact, Havering recorded the highest proportion of all London boroughs in 1991. This particular family type was also fairly widespread in the neighbouring districts of Thurrock, Barking and Dagenham and Redbridge. By contrast, however, married couples without any children were far less prevalent in inner London East. In 1991, Hackney had only 24

Table 6 Married couple families

London East	Total Families	Percentage of families comprising	
		Married couples with no children	Married couples with dependent child(ren)
Hackney	3,929	24.3	26.2
Tower Hamlets	3,537	25.3	30.0
Newham	5,777	26.0	34.7
Southwark	5,044	26.4	23.1
Lewisham	5,777	28.1	24.5
Greenwich	5,413	29.2	29.4
Waltham Forest	5,325	29.8	29.8
Thurrock	3,757	32.5	33.0
Barking&Dagenham	4,039	32.5	29.6
Redbridge	6,127	32.5	34.6
Bexley	6,205	33.4	33.0
Havering	6,719	35.2	32.7
Dartford	2,311	35.7	30.9
Greater London	166,540	30.7	30.4
Inner London	55,257	27.6	26.2
Outer London	111,283	32.2	32.6

Source: 10% sample data, 1991 Census, Crown Copyright.

per cent of married couple families, the lowest of all London boroughs. This is hardly surprising considering the low proportion of married residents living in Hackney. The proportion of families that were married couples without any children was equally way below the London average of 30.7 per cent in neighbouring Tower Hamlets, Southwark, Newham and Lewisham.

MARRIED COUPLE FAMILIES WITH DEPENDENT CHILD(REN)

A fairly similar London East pattern emerges with regards to the more traditional family of married couples with dependent children. Again, outer London East boroughs, particularly Redbridge, Thurrock, Bexley, Havering and Dartford, had a much higher proportion of traditional families in 1991. Nearly 35 per cent of all families were married couples with dependent children in Redbridge, the second highest of all London boroughs.[11] With regards to Barking and Dagenham and Greenwich, which had a high proportion of divorced residents in 1991, traditional families were less common. Here, the proportion of married couples with dependent children was below the London average and outer London average of 30.4 per cent and 32.6 per cent respectively. In relation to inner London East trends, both Newham and Tower Hamlets recorded a much higher proportion of traditional

families. Newham, for example, had the second highest proportion of married couple families with dependent children in the London East sub region. It is highly probable that the predominance of Asian communities has contributed to this particular trend. By contrast, the proportion of traditional families was exceptionally lower in Hackney, Lewisham and Southwark, way below the London average of 30.4 per cent. In Southwark, for example, only 23 per cent of families comprised married couples with dependent children, the lowest of all London boroughs, whilst just over a fifth were lone parent families. In fact, lone parent families similarly accounted for just over a fifth of all families in Hackney, compared to the London average of 11 per cent. In summary, traditional family forms have generally remained far more widespread in Outer London East. Let's look at trends in cohabitation.

COHABITATION

Over the past two decades, the popularity of cohabitation, as an alternative or precursor to marriage, has been rising steadily both internationally, nationally and regionally (Ditch *et al* 1996, Haskey 1996). As the 1991 Census of Population included a category for 'people living together' for the first time (Dale and Marsh, 1993), local patterns of cohabitation can now be explored. Throughout London as a whole, nearly 10 per cent of all London's families comprised of cohabiting couples, compared to the national average of 7.2 per cent. Cohabiting couples with dependent children were also above the national average in London, being much more widespread in inner London.[12] In relation to the London East sub region, cohabiting couples without dependent children were far more popular in inner London East. Lewisham, Southwark, Hackney and Tower Hamlets, for example, had over seven per cent of cohabiting couples compared with the London and national average of 6.9 per cent and 4.7 per cent respectively. The growth of professional and managerial workers (Rix 1997), and the in-migration of the new middle class (Porter 1994) may well be contributing to higher levels of cohabitation. By contrast, the proportion of families

Table 7   Cohabitation in London East

| | Percentage of families comprising | | |
London East	Total Families	Cohabiting couples with no children	Cohabiting couples with dependent child(ren)
Havering	6,719	3.9	1.6
Newham	5,777	4.7	2.7
Barking&Dagenham	4,039	4.8	3.4
Bexley	6,205	5.8	2.6
Greenwich	5,413	5.9	3.6
Redbridge	6,127	5.9	2.0
Thurrock	3,757	6.3	2.7
Dartford	2,311	6.5	3.1
Waltham Forest	5,325	7.1	2.9
Tower Hamlets	3,537	7.2	2.6
Hackney	3,929	7.4	3.4
Southwark	5,044	7.6	3.6
Lewisham	5,777	8.2	3.3
Greater London	166,540	6.9	2.6
Inner London	55,257	8.4	3.0
Outer London	111,283	6.2	2.4

Source; 10% sample data, 1991 Census, Crown Copyright

comprising couples living together without dependent children was below the London and Outer London average in Havering, Bexley, Barking and Dagenham, Redbridge and Greenwich in 1991.

UNMARRIED COUPLES WITH DEPENDENT CHILD(REN)

Interestingly, cohabiting couple families with dependent children were more common in the two outer London East boroughs of Greenwich and Barking and Dagenham. This was similarly the case in Southwark, Lewisham and Hackney. In 1991, for example, nearly four per cent of all families comprised of cohabiting couples with dependent children in both Greenwich and Southwark, the second and third highest proportion of all London boroughs.[13] Living together unmarried with dependent children, however, was far less common in the outer London East localities of Havering and Redbridge. Here, only 1.6 per cent and 2 per cent of families were cohabiting couples with children, the lowest of all London boroughs in 1991.[14] In summary, 'new' family forms, such as cohabiting couples with and without dependent children, were much more widespread in inner London East. Barking and Dagenham, Greenwich and Waltham Forest, however, diverged from the outer London East pattern, recording a higher proportion of cohabiting families with dependent children. The

next section of this paper examines the prevalence of other new patterns of family life and household composition in London East.

BIRTHS OUTSIDE OF MARRIAGE

The declining popularity of marriage and the widespread increase in cohabitation have contributed to the dramatic rise in having children outside of marriage. Nationally, for example, nearly a third of all births occurred outside of wedlock in 1994 compared to only eight per cent in 1970 (Ditch *et al* 1996). The impact of cohabitation, however, has been strikingly high. Of all UK births outside of marriage in 1994, over 75 per cent were in fact jointly registered, whilst over half were to couples living together at the same address (Haskey 1994). Having children outside of marriage has also rapidly increased throughout London as a whole, and all local London East districts. In London, whereas only 12 per cent of births took place outside of marriage in 1974, over twenty years later this had nearly trebled to 33.1 per cent. In 1995, just over half of those births were registered to cohabiting couples in London, whilst a large proportion were in fact to single mothers (*Focus on London* 1997).

Throughout the 1980s and 1990s, London East boroughs have similarly experienced a substantial increase in the proportion of births outside of marriage. Interestingly, the pace of

142

change has been far more rapid in the outer London East localities. In Havering and Bexley, for example, the proportion of births outside of marriage increased from around 10 per cent in 1983 to over 30 per cent twelve years later. The neighbouring boroughs of Barking and Dagenham, Greenwich and Redbridge similarly recorded an exceptionally high increase. In 1983, whereas only 17.1 per cent and 22.5 per cent of births were outside of wedlock in Barking and Dagenham and Greenwich, by 1995, this had more than doubled to over 40 per cent. Nearly a quarter of all births were to unmarried mothers in Redbridge by 1995, compared with only 9.4 per cent in 1983.

London East variations have remained. In 1995, for example, Southwark had nearly half of all births occurring outside of marriage, the highest of all London boroughs and well above the London average of 33.1 per cent. Over two-fifths of all births were also to unmarried mothers in the bordering locality of Lewisham, and Hackney, across the River Thames. Having children outside of marriage, however, was far less popular for women living in Tower Hamlets; religious and cultural diversity in relation to marriage and child-bearing are probably major contributing factors. On examining recent data,

Graph 2 Proportion of live births outside of marriage, London East

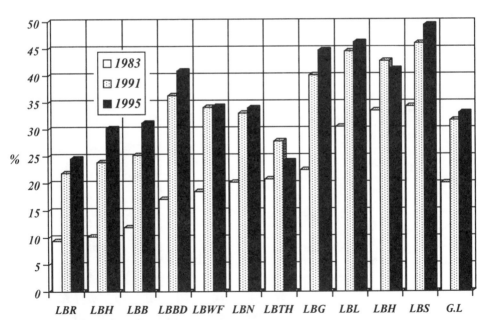

LBR=Redbridge, LBH=Havering, LBB=Bexley, LBBD=Barking&Dagenham, LBWF=Waltham Forest,
LBN=Newham, LBTH=Tower Hamlets, LBG=Greenwich, LBL=Lewisham, LBH=Hackney,
LBS=Southwark, G.L=Greater London

perhaps the most revealing trend is the divergence of Greenwich and Barking and Dagenham. Unlike outer London East neighbours, both localities had a high proportion of births outside of marriage, similar to that of Hackney, Lewisham and Southwark.

The growing popularity of cohabitation is apparent when examining more recent data on local births (Focus on London, 1997). Although outer London East boroughs have experienced a dramatic increase in children born outside of marriage, a strikingly high proportion were registered to cohabiting couples. In 1995, over 60 per cent of those births were registered to couples living together in Barking and Dagenham, Bexley and Havering, well exceeding the London and Outer London average of 52 per cent and 57.7 per

cent respectively. The adjacent neighbourhoods of Waltham Forest, Redbridge and Greenwich, also, had over half of all births outside of marriage registered to cohabiting couples. By contrast, however, more than 50 per cent of births were registered to single mothers in the inner London East boroughs of Newham, Hackney, Tower Hamlets, Southwark and Lewisham. Lone parent households, therefore, are far more prevalent.

LONE PARENT FAMILIES AND LONE PARENT HOUSEHOLDS IN LONDON EAST

Perhaps the most significant change within the composition of families over the past twenty-five years, however, has been the substantial growth of lone parent family households. Primarily as

Graph 3 Increasing proportion of lone parent households, London East

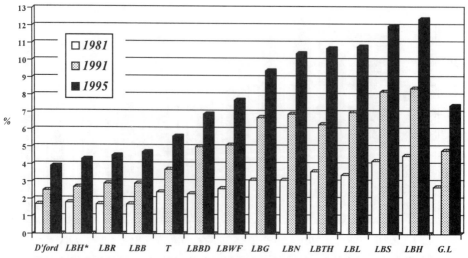

D'ford=Dartford, LBH* = Havering, LBR=Redbridge, LBB=Bexley, T=Thurrock, LBBD=Barking&Dagenham, LBWF=Waltham Forest, LBG=Greenwich, LBN=Newham, LBTH=Tower Hamlets, LBL=Lewisham, LBS=Southwark, LBH=Hackney, G.L=Greater London

a result of divorce, and more recently, having children outside of marriage, lone parent households have more than doubled in Britain. Whereas only three per cent of British households were lone parent households in 1971, this had risen to seven per cent by 1994. Not surprisingly, therefore, just over a fifth of all families with dependent children were headed by lone parents compared to only 8.6 per cent in 1971 (*Social Trends* 1997, Haskey 1996). Since the early 1980s, lone parent households have similarly increased throughout London and London East. Whereas lone parent households accounted for 2.7 per cent of all London households in 1981, by 1995, this had more than doubled to 7.4 per cent.

Turning to local variations, the number of lone parent households has also more than doubled in all London East boroughs. Since 1981, however, the rate of change has been far more pronounced in inner London East. Although Newham, Tower Hamlets and Lewisham had just three per cent of lone parent households in 1981, by 1995 this had risen to over 10 per cent. Throughout the same period, the proportion of lone parent households more than doubled in Southwark and Hackney. By 1995, both boroughs had around 12 per cent of lone parent households, the second and third highest of all London boroughs.[15] At the other end of the scale, however, lie the outer suburban districts of Dartford, Havering, Redbridge and Bexley. Here, although lone parent households have also doubled since 1981, those districts still had less than five per cent of households headed by lone parents in 1995. Lone parent households have, equally, more than doubled in the bordering neighbourhoods of Barking and Dagenham, Waltham Forest and Greenwich. By 1995, all inner London East boroughs, as well as Greenwich and Waltham Forest, recorded an above London average proportion of lone parent households.

Perhaps an even more striking indicator of changing family life is the growing proportion of dependent children living within lone parent family households. Nationally, just over a fifth of all dependent children were living in lone parent households in 1995 compared with a mere eight per cent in 1971. Exploring London East trends, the proportion of dependent children living in lone parent households dramatically increased in Southwark, Lewisham, Greenwich and Hackney. By 1991, over a quarter of dependent children were living in lone parent households in Hackney and Lewisham, compared with nearly a third in Southwark. Whereas Greenwich had only nine per cent of dependent children living in lone parent households in 1981, by 1991 this had dramatically increased to over a fifth. Despite the slight increase, Dartford, Havering and Redbridge had less than 10 per cent of dependent children in lone parent

Graph 4 Increasing proportion of dependent children living in lone parent households, London East

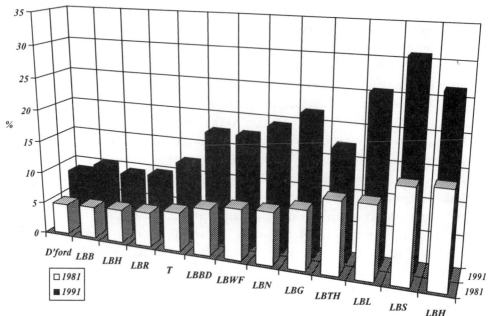

households, compared with only 12.2 per cent in Thurrock. Graph 4 shows the impact of changing family forms.

NEW LABOUR AND WELFARE TO WORK

Considering the widespread poverty and deprivation experienced by lone parents and their children, those particular trends are highly significant for future family and social security policy. Focusing on welfare to work, despite the back bench rebellion of December 1997 and widespread public disapproval, New Labour will remove lone parent benefits for new claimants and at the same time freeze benefit rates for existing claimants[16] from April this year. This will, essentially, reduce the living standards of around 2.5 million children by eight per cent

(Roberts 1997). Already, 58 per cent of lone parents with dependent children are living on incomes 50 per cent below the national average compared with just under a fifth in 1979 (Barclay 1995, Bradshaw 1996). In 1995, over 70 per cent of all lone parents were dependent on benefit (Flatley 1997). It is hardly surprising, therefore, that around 50 per cent of lone parents actually live on less than £100 per week compared with a mere four per cent of married couples (Roberts 1997). The removal of lone parent benefits for new claimants will clearly exacerbate levels of childhood poverty in a country which already has one of the highest childhood[17] poverty rates in Europe. If the rising number of lone parent family households continues throughout London East,

146

particularly inner London East, New Labour's social security legislation will have serious implications!

What are some of the implications for existing lone parent claimants? Using £3.2 billion from a private utilities windfall tax, welfare to work, aims to get lone parents, as well as young people unemployed, the long term unemployed and the disabled and long term sick back into work, education or training. At present, the New Deal will target only lone parents on benefit whose youngest child is of school age. The scheme aims to help lone parents back into work, education or training by providing advice and support on financial issues, child-care and job searching at the local job centre (Flatley 1997). Whilst the basic principle of assisting lone parents to find work may be welcomed, two fundamental criticisms centre around the issue of 'compulsion' and 'what type of jobs'? (Deacon and Mann 1997, Roberts 1997). Looking at the issue of 'compulsion', the New Deal scheme for lone parents is currently voluntary, unlike for those young people unemployed and the long term unemployed. There is, however, a possibility of New Labour implementing a future benefit penalty clause for lone parents failing to take up opportunities once their child begins school (Brindle 1997). A possible reduction of benefit will again have serious implications for lone parents and their children already living in financial hardship.

Focusing on London East, over 90 per cent of all lone parents were women, whilst over two-thirds were not in employment in 1991 (Dartford was an exception; 10.1 per cent of lone parents were male and over 40 per cent were working). Given the current lack of job opportunities for local people without any qualifications or skills, it is hard to imagine a scenario whereby all lone parents who want to work will actually find jobs in London East, a region hard hit by industrial decline and economic restructuring (Rix 1996, 1997). This is similarly the case for all groups targetted by the New Deal, which are disproportionately represented in London as a whole (Flatley 1997), particularly eastern areas (Rix 1997). Again, the implications are immense! Examining the social geography of 'work poor' households also shows the impact of widespread economic change throughout the London East sub region.

'WORK POOR' HOUSEHOLDS

Since the 1970s, industrial decline and economic restructuring have certainly led to periods of high unemployment and widespread job insecurity throughout Britain (Hutton 1995). In relation to London East, particularly inner localities, the continuing shift towards a predominantly service sector economy and labour market deregulation have clearly resulted in a rapid loss of full-time male

Map 2: Proportion of households with no adult in employment, London East 1991.

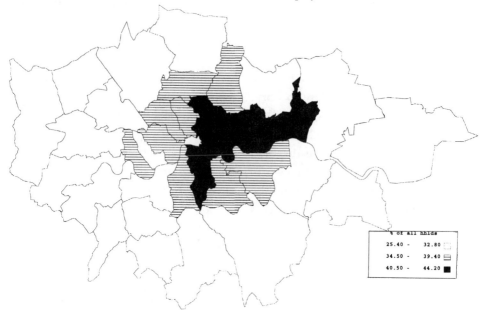

Map 3: Proportion of households with two or more adults in employment, London East 1991.

148

employment (Rix, 1996, 1997). Throughout the 1980s, both economic inactivity and unemployment for young people and ethnic minority residents also increased. Along with national and London wide trends, the proportion of households without any adults in employment similarly increased in all London East districts between 1981 and 1991. Although Havering, Greenwich and Barking and Dagenham recorded the highest percentage increase, by 1991 'work poor' households remained far more prevalent in inner London East boroughs. For example, Tower Hamlets, Hackney, Southwark and Newham had over two-fifths of households without any adults working, way above the London average of 34 per cent, and the highest of all London boroughs. Barking and Dagenham also had over 40 per cent of 'work poor' households, nearly 10 per cent higher than the Outer London average, and the highest of all Outer London boroughs. By contrast, neighbouring outer London East boroughs had a far lower proportion of 'work poor' households. This was especially the case in Dartford, where only 28 per cent of households had no adults in employment. Mapping London-wide variations clearly show the disproportionate share of households without any adult in employment in inner London localities.

The inner and outer London pattern is reversed when examining the social geography of households with two or more adults in employment (see Map.3). The proportion of households with two or more adult earners was generally much higher in all outer London boroughs. This is not surprising considering the higher proportion of women generally economically active and in paid work in Outer London. Exploring London East trends, considerable dissimilarities are apparent. For example, whereas 41 per cent and 39 per cent of households had two or more adults working in Dartford and Redbridge, the respective proportions for Hackney and Tower Hamlets were just over a fifth. All inner London East localities recorded a below London average proportion of two or more earner households of 32 per cent in 1991. This was also the case in Barking and Dagenham and Greenwich. In summary, the inner and outer London East divergence has clearly emerged with regards to both work poor households and households with two or more earners. During a period of industrial decline, economic transformation and limited labour market opportunities, New Labour's commitment to reshaping the welfare state around the principle of the work ethic (Witcher 1997) will certainly have widespread implications for local people living in London East, especially inner areas.

SINGLE PERSON HOUSEHOLDS

Another major trend contributing to the diversity of household structure, both national and European-wide, has been the widespread growth of single person households. Along with ageing, both marital decline and divorce have also contributed to this expansion (Ditch *et al* 1996). By 1995, over 28 per cent of British households contained one adult only compared with less than a fifth in 1971. Throughout the 1980s and 1990s, the trend of living alone had also impacted on London and London East. Whereas a quarter of all London households were single person households in 1981, by 1995 this had risen to 33 per cent.

Single person households have also become much more widespread in all London East boroughs. Geographically, however, the pace of change has been rather varied. Between 1981 and 1995, for example, Southwark, Havering, Waltham Forest, Tower Hamlets, Greenwich and Dartford experienced an above London average increase in households containing only one adult. In Havering, the proportion of single person households rose from 16.7 per cent in 1981 to 25.1 per cent in 1995. Despite the general increase, the inner London East localities tend to have a higher proportion of single person households. In 1995, for example, over

Table 8 Single person households

| London East | One person households as a % of all households | | | |
	1981	1991	1995	81 - 95 % increase
Thurrock	16.0	22.1	23.3	7.3
Havering	16.7	22.8	25.1	8.4
Dartford	17.4	22.9	25.0	7.6
Bexley	18.5	24.1	25.4	6.9
Redbridge	22.0	26.9	28.6	6.6
Barking&Dagenham	21.9	27.4	28.9	7.0
Waltham Forest	24.5	30.6	32.3	7.8
Greenwich	23.7	29.9	31.4	7.7
Newham	23.6	29.2	29.4	5.8
Lewisham	25.6	33.0	32.6	7.0
Tower Hamlets	28.9	35.5	36.5	7.6
Hackney	30.0	36.1	36.2	6.2
Southwark	29.4	36.7	37.6	8.2
London	26.0	31.9	33.0	7.0

Source: 1981 and 1991 Census, Crown Copyright; *Regional Trends* 1997.

150

Graph 5 Lone pensioner households, London East

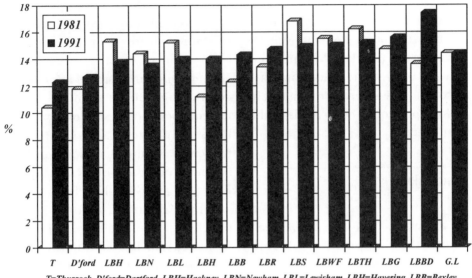

□ *1981*
■ *1991*

%

T   D'ford LBH LBN LBL LBH LBB LBR LBS LBWF LBTH LBG LBBD G.L

T=Thurrock, D'ford=Dartford, LBH=Hackney, LBN=Newham, LBL=Lewisham, LBH=Havering, LBB=Bexley,
LBR=Redbridge, LBS=Southwark, LBWF=Waltham Forest, LBTH=Tower Hamlets, LBG=Greenwich,
LBBD=Barking&Dagenham, G.L=Greater London

a third of all households contained only one person in Tower Hamlets, Hackney and Southwark, the only London East boroughs exceeding the London average of 33 per cent. Both Lewisham, Greenwich and Waltham Forest also had over 30 per cent of single person households, nearly 10 per cent higher than that found in Thurrock.

LONE PENSIONER HOUSEHOLDS

Drawing on the 1981 and 1991 Censuses, lone pensioner households also increased in all outer London East localities, apart from Waltham Forest. Not surprisingly, Barking and Dagenham, a predominantly stable white working-class community with a large elderly population, recorded

the highest increase in single pensioner households. By 1991, lone pensioner households accounted for nearly a fifth of all households in Barking and Dagenham, way above the London average of 14.4 per cent. Both Greenwich and Redbridge, as well as Tower Hamlets and Southwark, similarly recorded an above London average proportion of single pensioner households. The increasing number of elderly residents living alone, however, has not been a uniform trend. Inner London East localities, for example, experienced a slight decline in lone pensioner households throughout the 1980s. The high proportion of ethnic minority residents, who are generally younger, and the lower than average proportion of elderly residents may well have contributed to this trend. As London's ethnic minority elderly population is expected to rise from around 70, 000 to 126,000 over the next decade (Storkey, Maguire and Lewis 1997), inner London East boroughs may well record an increase in lone pensioner households in the 2001 Census.

Conclusion

In summary, over the past fifteen years, the composition of both families and households has been under going fairly rapid change throughout the London East sub region. Although the pace of change has been highly variable, our sub region now has a complex set of family patterns and a diversity of household structures. Considerable borough variations, however, have remained. The outer London East districts of Bexley, Havering, Redbridge, Dartford and Thurrock, for example, generally have lower fertility rates, a lower proportion of young children, a higher proportion of married residents and married couple families. Cohabiting couple families, births outside of marriage, lone parent family households and single person households, although rising, have also remained lower when compared with inner London East. By contrast, new patterns of family and household formation were far more widespread in inner London East, as well as Barking and Dagenham and Greenwich. Those boroughs had higher fertility rates, larger numbers of young children and a higher proportion of divorced residents. Having children outside of marriage, cohabiting couple families with dependent children and lone parent households were also far more numerous. Living alone was equally far more popular in inner London East, along with Waltham Forest.

Throughout London East, therefore, both old and new traditions have been upheld, clearly illustrating the growing trend towards difference and diversity. The promotion of traditional family values, however, advocated by the previous Conservative government, and now under New Labour, seriously neglects widespread demographic and social change. Marital decline, divorce, remarriage, cohabitation, living alone, having children outside of marriage, as well as alternative gay lifestyles[18] are certainly 1990s traditions. Different and diverse, those traditions will lead Britain, London and London East into the next millennium. New Labour's forthcoming social policy agenda, therefore, needs to recognise the plurality of existing family forms and 'promote forms of welfare that enable individuals to respond to the challenges contemporary society throws at them' (Deacon and Mann 1997, p.6).

REFERENCES

Barclay, P. (1995), *Report of an Inquiry into Income and Wealth*, York: Joseph Rowntree Foundation.

Bradshaw, J. (1996), 'Family Policy and Family Poverty', *Policy Studies*, Vol. 17, No. 2.

Bradshaw, J. *et al* (1996), *Policy and Employment of Lone Parents in 20 countries*, York: SPRU.

Brindle, D.(1997), 'Making it work for lone parents', *The Guardian*, 31st December.

1981 Census, London: HMSO.

1991 Census, London: HMSO.

Dale, A. and C. Marsh (1993), *The 1991 Census User's Guide*, London: HMSO.

Deacon, A. and K. Mann (1997), 'Moralism and Modernity: The Paradox of New Labour Thinking on Welfare', *Benefits*, 2 September/October, .

Ditch, J., H. Barnes and J. Bradshaw (1996), *European Observatory on National Family Policies: A Synthesis of National Family Policies*, University of York: Social Policy Research Unit.

Edwards, R. and S. Duncan (1997), 'Supporting the family: lone mothers, paid work and the underclass debate', *Critical Social Policy, 17 (4): 29-49*.

Flatley, J. (1997), *Welfare to work: what does it mean for London?*, London: London Research Centre.

Harker, L. (1996), 'New Paths for Social Security', in A. Walker and C. Walker (eds), *Britain divided, The growth of social exclusion in the 1980s and 1990s*, London: CPAG.

Haskey, J. (1996), 'Population Review: Families and Households in Great Britain', *Population Trends*, 85.

Hutton, W. (1995), *The State We're In*, London: Jonathan Cape.

London Research Centre (1997), *Focus on London*, London: HMSO.

Millar, J. (1996), 'Gender', in A. Walker, and C. Walker (eds), *Britain divided: The growth of social exclusion in the 1980s and 1990s*, London: CPAG.

Porter, R. (1994), *A Social History of London*, London: Hamish Hamilton.

Pullinger, J. and C. Summerfield (eds) (1997), *Social Focus on Families*, London: Office for National Statistics.

Regional Trends, 1996, 1997, London: HMSO.

Rix, V. (1996), 'Social and demographic change in East London', in T. Butler and M. Rustin (eds), *Rising in the East: The Regeneration of East London*, London: Lawrence and Wishart.

Rix, V. (1997), 'Industrial decline, economic restructuring and social exclusion in London East throughout the 1980s and 1990s', *Rising East, a journal of East London Studies*, Issue 1, London: Lawrence and Wishart.

Roberts, Y. (1997), 'The way that lone parents really behave', *The Guardian, 9 December 1997*.

Rustin, M. (1997), 'What can a journal contribute to East London regeneration? Not so much a plan, as a Public Conversation', *Rising East*, 1; 2.

Ruxton, S. (1996), *Children in Europe*, NCH for Children.

Social Trends, 1997, London: HMSO.

Storkey, M. (1996), *One City, Many Communities*, Policy Studies Institute.

Storkey, M., J. Maguire and R. Lewis (1997), *Cosmopolitan London Past Present and Future*, London Research Centre.

Witcher, S. (1997), 'New Labour: thinking the unthinkable', *Poverty, 9*.

NOTES

1. Analysing family trends for local boroughs is hampered by the lack of comparative data. All aspects of change within the composition of families and households, therefore, cannot be provided.

2. The 1991 Census imputed data for missing households. In calculating population change, the 1981 propulation base has been used. Other aspects of change have been calculated using the 1991 population base. Difference in percentage points are, therefore, affected by the exclusion of absent households in 1981 population base.

3. Population information relates to the 1995 mid-year population estimates.

4. LRC projections are for London boroughs only. It is highly likely that Dartford and Thurrock also have less than 10 per cent of ethnic minority groups.

5. Total Period Fertility Rates measure the average number of children a woman would be expected to have if she experienced the age-specific rates of the year in question throughout her child-bearing life.

6. Britain still has one of the highest fertility rates in Europe.

7. In 1995, the Total Period Fertility Rate for Dartford and Thurrock was 1.81 and 1.84 respectively.

8. Changes within the age structure of woman, ethnicity and social class are significant contributing factors of fertility. A future Trends East issue will focus on family and household patterns for London East's ethnic minority population.

9. The 1991 Census of Population defined a family as 'consisting of at least two people who may be either married or living together as a couple and of the opposite sex, with or without never married children, or a parent living with his or her never married child(ren)' (Dale and Marsh, 1993, p.40).

10. Family composition data relates to a 10 per cent sample only.

11. Harrow had the highest proportion of married couple families with dependent children (35.6%).

12. Haskey (1996) found that cohabiting couple families with dependent children were also quite prevalent in some districts of Greater Manchester.

13. Camden had the highest proportion of families that were cohabiting couples with dependent children.

14. Only 1.6 per cent of families also comprised of cohabiting couples with dependent children in Harrow.

15. Lambeth, one of the pilot areas for Labour's New Deal scheme, had the highest proportion of lone parent households.

16. In April 1996, the Universal One Parent Benefit and Income Support Lone Parent Premium were frozen at current levels. Child Benefit was also frozen in 1987.

17. Latest figures from the Household below Average Income survey indicate

154

that the proportion of children living in poverty has risen from one in ten to one in three since 1979.

18. Unfortunately, large government surveys fail to include gay relationships or gay households.

National heterotopia:
Greenwich as spectacle, 1694-1869

Sarah Monks

As the creation of a national spectacle at the Millennium Dome site establishes its hold upon public imagination and debate, it seems apposite to examine earlier manifestations of Greenwich as a site of national significance.[1] Seen today perhaps as another part of London's sprawl, Greenwich, as experienced 'in the flesh' or vicariously through images and texts, nevertheless played a unique role in the creation and consolidation of social, political and national identities in this period. Its peculiar combination of symbolic spaces made it a potent site for the construction of national spectacle. Able to embody ideas about the nation, its past, present and future, Greenwich functioned within British culture as a heterotopia, as a kind of place 'outside of all places, even thought it may be possible to indicate [its] location in reality...' in which other places and times are represented and contested.[2] By looking at some of its promoted 'readings', this article will attempt to recover some idea of what Greenwich could signify to the British public in the eighteenth and nineteenth centuries.[3] In turn, I hope to highlight the extent to which the physical and artistic manipulation of built and 'natural' environments is always a charged process which, like all historical processes, bears the marks of contemporary debate.

GREENWICH HOSPITAL

In focusing on the medieval riverside Palace of Placentia and, from 1621, the Queen's House, the earliest images of Greenwich emphasise its royal character and its consequent use as a site of elite leisure. But its development as national spectacle began with the establishment and construction of Greenwich Hospital. This was a building project whose size, financial complexities and political implications would more than match those of its twentieth-century counterpart at Greenwich Peninsula. It is through organising

156

and overseeing the construction of public sites like Greenwich Hospital and, dare one say, the Millennium Dome, that political administrations are able both to give visual expression to their aims and ideologies and to shape public response to their actions. So what did Greenwich Hospital 'say' to its earliest viewers?

The hospital conveyed an important message about the revised relationship between crown and subject in the late seventeenth century. With the exile to France of the Catholic sympathiser James II, the 1688 accession of his son-in-law and daughter, William and Mary, was facilitated by a congeries of financial, political and religious interests keen to establish a new-style Protestant monarchy. Crucially, the power of this monarchy over Parliament and public finance was to be limited both by a reappraisal of the legitimisation of royal power[4] and by new public institutions such as the Bank of England. Whilst the idea of a public hospital for sailors had been touted for some years, it was Queen Mary who decided in 1694 to donate the riverside grounds of the old royal palace and to insist upon the incorporation of Charles II's unfinished palace wing (begun there by Sir Christopher Wren, who was then charged with overseeing the construction of Greenwich Hospital itself) into the new building plans.[5] The symbolism of this gesture - the

Figure 1: Thomas Bowles, Greenwich Hospital, *coloured engraving, 1745. National Maritime Museum, Greenwich (PAF7639)*

incorporation of an historically-charged site of royal power with the establishment of a public institution which would promote the benefits of 'the Trade, Navigation and Naval Strength of this Our Realm of England (whereupon the Safety and flourishing State thereof does so much depend)'[6] - is potent. Combined with the fact that the financing of the hospital was expressly to be a matter for both the crown and its subjects,[7] this gesture suggested not only that the new-style monarchy was desirous of acting in the public good, but that this end was best served by a collaboration between royal and public powers - an effective analogy of the state's post-1688 structure.

The symbolism of the hospital's establishment carries over into its architectural and artistic representations. Taking his cue from his earlier palace wing, Wren's design for the hospital is magnificently palatial[8] - indeed, it is the grandest scheme of his career, employing the stylistic language and spatial forms of the Italian renaissance palace to construct an architectural spectacle of regal immensity. The orientation of the site is however emphatically public, opening out onto the 'street' of the Thames, the commercial gateway to the nation, quasi-urban in its social diversity. The hospital was thus addressed to both upstream London and the English people at large, and

from the late 1690s it was represented in topographical prints whose proliferation suggests that sections of the public understood the hospital as a site of interest and relevance to them, despite (or perhaps because of) its royal appearance (figure 1).

By combining the cartographer's concern with the mapping and fixing of space with an emphasis upon the pictorial effects of spatial recession and single-point perspective, these prints suggest the hospital's origins in discourses of geometry and rational knowledge. In using this pictorial mode and a distant viewpoint which allows the viewer to command the spectacle, these prints therefore suggest that the hospital can be understood and viewed in its entirety, and this by a broad public. Since although both the commanding viewpoint and the topographical mode have their English origins in the representation of the private landed estate, the separation here of the viewer from the land surveyed lessens the proprietorial implications of these devices, and allows the hospital to appear a truly public spectacle. The foreground representation of river transport, and the inclusion of hospital visitors, reinforces the reading of this as a grand but clearly public space, expressive of a new relationship between crown and subject.

Moreover, Thomas Bowles's

engraving, made fifty years after the hospital's initiation but still some six years away from its completion, places it beside the clutter of Greenwich town. Although radically different stylistically and spatially, these two elements of the built landscape of Greenwich are nevertheless shown to co-exist. Symbolic of the supposed harmonious unity of the English state, Bowles' representation of the hospital amongst private dwellings is also expressive of the peculiar character of the English 'liberty' secured in 1688. With great artistic licence, this London printmaker pulls the hospital forward from the riverbank so that it appears as a great bulwark, metaphorically shoring up and protecting the town, and, by implication, the nation beyond, from invasion and overturn. In this way the print gives visual expression to the contemporary idea that the protection and progress of the English nation, and its increasing outposts, was best served by the new manifestation of the state.

Whilst Greenwich Hospital, in its construction and in its many representations, could embody the reformation of the state apparatus, so it was also a massive statement of intent regarding the new state's conception of itself on the world stage. Established in direct response to the heavy casualties from the 1692 battle of La Hogue (when an attempt by Louis XIV to invade England and regain the throne for James II was crushed by the Anglo-Dutch fleet), the hospital was to 'encrease the Number of English Seamen' and strengthen 'Our Navy Royall' by 'making some Competent Provision, That Seamen, who by Age, Wounds or other Accidents, shall become Disabled... may not fall under Hardships and Miseries'.[9] In effect then, the hospital's establishment was a highly visible promise that England was committed to its own defence. It was also, in its commitment to increasing naval resources, a bombastic statement to viewers at home and abroad (especially in France) that England was entering the European military arena from which it had previously refrained. Indeed, the following century would prove to be the longest period of English involvement in warfare since the middle ages. Where England had, in the centuries since then, been a marginal power, unwilling and unable to participate in large-scale European warfare, its attitude to foreign affairs and to its own position in the hierarchy of world power was to be radically revised from the late seventeenth century with the institution of the new 'fiscal-military' state.[10] From 1689, the state's commitment to waging war was such that it would become the largest single employer in the nation as the inflation of the navy became the major goal of public expenditure.[11] Issuing from England's political resolve, this naval drive was also central to the nation's trading aspirations, as is clear from the explicit link made in the hospital's establishment, between the strengthening of the navy and 'the Supplying and Carrying on the Occasions and Business of Our Merchants, and other Our Loving Subjects, Interested in Trade, Commerce, Fishing, Plantation, Discovery...'.[11] Greenwich Hospital was important therefore in communicating a new conception of England as an agent in world affairs.

Equally, the hospital can be seen as a riposte to those who feared that William's bellicose policies were the result of his own personal dynastic ambitions. Since a return to the iniquities of the old rule and its attachments to the old enemy (France) seems to have been the universal fear for the English, it is telling that the hospital was established in the aftermath of the one conflict which secured England against the immediate threats of Catholic monarchy and French invasion. Greenwich Hospital was therefore a highly public statement that this new 'fiscal-military' state aimed to secure English liberties and was specifically national in intention. Altogether it is, then, the most spectacular visual expression of the English state's transformation in the late seventeenth century.

GREENWICH PARK

Whilst the spectacle of Greenwich Hospital continued to signify notions of the state throughout the period, the town's other major attraction, Greenwich Park and, crucially, its view over the capital city beyond, played an increasingly important role in ideological debate. Indeed, the view from the park was central to the depiction of London during this period, for in its ability to provide a richly-significant frame to the city view, Greenwich Park became a prime site in landscape art of the eighteenth and nineteenth centuries. By examining some of its images, we can begin to understand how the park, as represented and perhaps even as experienced, could inform contemporary debate.

Until at least 1832, the landed aristocracy was considered solely qualified for political office and suffrage, a rule whose justification lay in the belief that, with the intellectual liberties provided by a life of independent means, it was the landed class alone who were capable of conceiving the public good. The dominance of this ideology meant that the claims to political representation of those (non-aristocratic, urban) men of commercial means were rejected (although considered increasingly legitimate through the late eighteenth and early nineteenth

Figure 2: Stevens after Pieter Tillemans, A View of London and Wesminster, &c, from One Tree Hill, Greenwich Park, etching 1752. National Maritime Museum, Greenwich. (PAF 7620).

centuries) on the basis that their political motives could only be borne of self-interest and desire for profit. Equally, it was argued that the palpable investment of landed men (for it was only men) in the very soil of the nation resulted in a civic and moral fixity far superior to the seeming value-system of commercial men, whose investment lay rather in mobile and exchangeable commodities. Since land, and its distinction from the city, was therefore such a defining issue, landscape images were important in consolidating and contesting ideas about political representation.[13]

The dominant modes of British landscape art in this period derived from the image of the country estate and an aesthetic legitimisation of the dominant landed ideology. Landscape images emphasised the estate's rural 'nature' (naturalising the social inequalities which facilitated and maintained it) and its beauty (proving by analogy the moral virtue of its owners). The epitome, in this aesthetic, of the unnatural and unlovely, the cityscape with all its social and moral ambiguities could present an ideological threat to the very basis of a British landscape imagery. Both Turner's print (figure 2) and the poem which accompanied his original oil painting in 1809 express the incompatibility of the city with the traditional landscape aesthetic:

> Where burthen'd Thames reflects the crowded sail,
> Commercial care and busy toils prevail,
> Whose murky veil, aspiring to the skies,
> Obscures thy beauty, and thy form denies,
> Save where thy spires pierce the doubtful air,
> As gleams of hope amidst a world of care.

It is telling that this is one of very few images of London by this major British landscape artist of the early nineteenth century. Employing a landscape mode to represent the cityscape, and so the spaces and values of a new urban economic order, was highly problematic.[14]

In this respect, the view from Greenwich Park was something of a godsend for artists throughout this period, for it prefaced the city with the signs and symbols of hierarchy and tradition. A visual trope developed in which the viewer, by extension a member of the polite society around him, marvels at the metropolis from the safety of this rural estate-like landscape (figure 3). The cityscape beyond,[15] filtered by the connotations of social hierarchy and moral virtue allowed by the park's

Figure 3: Charles Turner after Joseph Mallord William Turner, London, from Greenwich, *mezzotint etching, 1811. National Maritime Museum, Greenwich. (PAF3270)*

Arty Facts

rural character, was thus rescued from its own dangerous implications - to the extent that women, more vulnerable to the city's vices, are commonly shown as spectators beside men. Equally, London's contentious modernity is countered by the foreground trappings of a royal park (complete with deer and oak trees) in a 'reading' of the city which privileges historical precedent and tradition. An uncompromising spectacle for its beholder, this was one of the few city views which could secure one's social, political and moral personality against the threats of capital. The view from the park reinforced arguments that the city could not be represented (whether visually or politically) on its own terms, and that its comprehension was the reserve of those who, untainted by contact with the urban world of commerce, could survey the scene from a position of landed tradition and moral virtue. Turner's image augments this last point further by isolating the viewer from any immediate signs of urban society. Alone, save for grazing deer, the viewer looks out through the foliage as if gazing into a hellish future from some antediluvian idyll. Here, the moral and aesthetic contradistinction of city and country ideologies was made complete.

HETEROTOPIA

In the battle to maintain and uphold the status quo, Greenwich Park was therefore an important site - especially in the early nineteenth century, when its representation took on a new urgency as alternative claims to political power grew increasingly vocal. The ability of Greenwich as spectacle to communicate the liberty and 'naturalness' of the British constitution, through hospital and park views respectively, gave it a special significance in the struggle against democracy's artificial conception of political rights. Amongst it all tottered the figure of the Greenwich Pensioner. Subjected to a disciplined regime, humiliating punishment, a tiny allowance and a life of unenviable boredom, the pensioner's representation nevertheless as cheerful local character suggests that his was a figure through which the myth of a controlled and contented poor could be maintained. Like Greenwich as a whole, the pensioner became both spectacle and cultural artefact - a major attraction for tourists until his final departure in 1869:

On a fine day, the old pensioners may be seen in every direction, rambling about the park, in which they appear to find much delight.... Some of these old heroes have lost a leg, others an arm... yet they go stomping about as happy, to all appearance, as the credulous stranger whom they delight to cram with some true sailors 'yarn'.[16]

Central to this fascination with the pensioner was his status as embodiment of living history and of the moral value of patriotic self-sacrifice. The lessons in respect for tradition and duty which his image could impart to a politically-active middle class consolidated Greenwich's increasing role as repository of a particular version of British history (figure 4). In 1824, the hospital's Naval Gallery was opened - a space in which the portraits, biographies and shining moments of a litany of high-ranking naval heroes were presented for public edification.[17] One of the first museums of a national scope, its emphasis upon chronology and seniority in the narration of British history was important in communicating a hierarchical, tradition-bound slant on the past to a broad public.[18]

Altogether, Greenwich as spectacle could provide the viewer/visitor with a homogeneous set of visual experiences, whose significance lay precisely in their ability to communicate key ideas about the nation at times of change. As I have outlined them, these ideas - about the monarchy, the aristocracy, and the middle classes - were central to the establishment and maintenance of a concept of national unity. Greenwich therefore had an important role to play in expressing, exalting and preserving

Figure 4: T Holles after Edward Matthew Ward, The Greenwich Pensioner, *etching and engraving, 1845. National Maritime Museum, Greenwich. (PAH3306)*

Arty Facts

the very values upon which elite hopes for national unity were founded, and although threatened during the late eighteenth and early nineteenth centuries, these values still operate effectively at the level of myth today. As construction of the Millennium Dome progresses, the character of the spectacle with which Greenwich will be endowed will continue to play an important role in informing and constructing concepts of British identity.

NOTES

1. My emphasis will be upon the nexus of sites which comprised tourist Greenwich during this period, centring on the Royal Hospital for Seamen (hereafter referred to as Greenwich Hospital) and Greenwich Park.

2. Foucault, M. (1985/6) Of Other Spaces: Utopias and Heterotopias. *Lotus* 48/9: pp9-17.

3. Throughout, my discussion will be led by the methodological assumption that, whilst historical human experience is irretrievable as such, an analysis of cultural artefacts can help us to understand the frames of reference which guide and condition expectation and experience. I am aware, however, that we cannot unthinkingly elide suggested experience (as read through prints and texts) with actual experience - it is more than likely for example that the ordered progression through Greenwich suggested by nineteenth-century guidebooks such as Clarke, H. G. (1852) *The Pictorial Guide to Greenwich. A Holiday Handbook.* London: H. G. Clarke was far from realised in reality.

4. Where Parliament had granted James II life competency in the form of a continuous yield from indirect taxes, which he then set about maximising, William and Mary were merely granted four-year periods of such competency and the maximising reforms of James II were curbed. In this way, the financial independence of the crown was terminated, and the calling of regular Parliaments assured. See Brewer, J. (1989) *The Sinews of Power: War, Money and the English State.* London: Unwin Hyman, pp.144-5. My discussion of the construction of a new state is deeply indebted to this excellent book.

5. Merwe, P. van der (1994) *'A Refuge for All': Greenwich Hospital, 1694-1994.* London: National Maritime Museum in association with Greenwich Hospital, p.1.

6. William III (1695) *Commission for Greenwich Hospital*, p.6.

7. The financial history of Greenwich hospital was, however, less than exemplary in its embodiment of the relationship between crown and subjects. Whilst William promised an annual grant of £2,000, his inability to dedicate this sum is suggested by the fact that no royal monies were received until 1697, when he bequeathed the sum as credits against the (deeply unpopular) malt tax, repealed in 1700. Equally, the hospital was not overwhelmed with private bequests, and some of those that it did receive were later reneged on. Ultimately, much of the hospital's funds came from a combination of smuggling fines, sequestered estates (in particular, those of the pirate Captain Kidd and the Jacobite Earl of Derwentwater), sailors's welfare payments and parliamentary grants. See Merwe, P. van der (1994), p.2. The hospital's financial problems resulted in the disjointed progress of building works which was barely

represented in images of the site.

8. Too much so for some critics, who felt that the institution's grand aspect jarred with its charitable scope. This tension between its aims (and, more specifically, its poor decrepit inhabitants) and its appearance was a constant theme in discussions of the Hospital.

9. William III (1695), pp.6-7.

10. The phrase is Brewer's and refers to the new character of the state, as developed in the late seventeenth century, in which a 'radical increase in taxation, the development of public deficit finance on an unprecedented scale, and the growth of a sizeable public administration devoted to organising the fiscal and military activities of the state' were combined. See Brewer, J. (1989), p.xvii.

11. Of all European powers, except Holland, England spent the highest proportion of its public expenditure on naval development and infrastructure - altogether, the costs of military engagement in the century after 1688 would account for around 75% of public spending. England's ability to do this was in part due to its earlier abstention from sustained warfare. See Brewer, J (1989), pp.26-41.

12. William III (1695), p.7.

13. See Bermingham, A. (1986) *Landscape and Ideology: The English Rustic Tradition*. Berkeley and Los Angeles: University of California Press; Barrell, J. (1990) The Public Prospect and the Private View: The Politics of Taste in Eighteenth-Century Britain.

14. See Potts, A. (1988) Picturing the Modern Metropolis: Images of London in the Nineteenth Century. *History Workshop* 26: 28-56, and Hemingway, A. (1992) *Landscape Imagery and Urban Culture in Early Nineteenth-Century Britain*.

Cambridge: Cambridge University Press.

15. The early nineteenth-century landscape artist's retreat to Greenwich seems an important rebuttal of contemporary claims that the city was now too sprawling to be commanded visually from any one viewpoint and could only really be experienced visually through series of street-level views. See Potts, A. (1988) and Helsinger, E. K. (1997), p.16.

16. Clarke, H. G. (1860) *Greenwich Hospital; the Park and Picture Gallery. A Hand-Book Guide for Visitors*. London: H. G. Clarke, p.14.

17. Since 1705, and the arrival of the first pensioner, members of the public had been able to visit certain areas of the hospital in return for a fee. The Naval Gallery was originally open during weekdays and charged its visitors - its opening to the public for free and at weekends from 1843 was hailed as a great step in the drive to educate the taste and sentiments of the masses. See Clarke (1852), *Greenwich Hospital; its Painted Hall and Chapel. A Hand-Book Guide for Visitors*. London: H. G. Clarke, p.vii.

18. See the forthcoming publication on the history of the Naval Gallery and, as it would become, the National Maritime Museum by Kevin Littlewood and Beverly Butler, to be published by Athlone Press in association with the National Maritime Museum. My thanks to Margarette Lincoln for allowing me to read the text in manuscript draft.

Tower Hamlets's street life: generations apart

Rehan Jamil

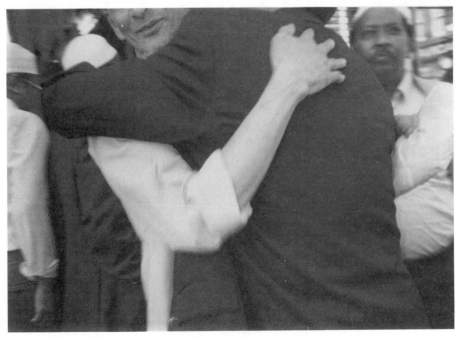

East End fictions

Richard McKeever

Jack London was one of the most imaginative of the Victorian urban explorers and his *People of the Abyss* one of the most influential texts in the genre. Recently a team of artists in residence worked with year 10 pupils from Morpeth School in Bethnal Green on a project using photography to re-examine critically the significance of Jack London's work from the standpoint of their own contemporary experience of the areas he depicted a century ago. In this interview with John Marriott and Phil Cohen, Daniel Rubenstein and Oreet Ashery describe the strategies they used in working with the young people and how the project relates to their own pre-occupations as immigrants and artists. This is followed by an account by Tim Brennan on the thinking behind his 'performed walks' around East London, and the creative strategies he uses to deconstruct stereotypes of the area and its populations. The interview began with a question to Daniel Rubenstein about his choice of the Jack London book.

Daniel Rubenstein: I first came across Jack London when I was a seven or eight year-old in Russia. In Russia Jack London was very popular, because he is one of the few American so-called socialist writers. I had 14 volumes of his books, more than you get in English! The letters, an enormous amount of articles for the socialist press, everything. Even very weird stuff like hunting for slaves in the Pacific.

I was reading him in Leningrad as a child, when I came across *People of the Abyss*, and I remember the feeling he describes of a totally foreign place, a place where personally I had never been. It happened that I found myself living in England 20 years later, walking in the same streets that he described, I felt a very strong urge to re-read the book with the geographical knowledge of the same streets. When I re-read it I realised it was a great piece of work, an amazing documentary and literary achievement. I began wondering what one could do with it. I thought about making a play, or taking photographs, and then this idea came together with Camerawork, and Morpeth School, to do a project which would involve children.

You had this strong mental image from reading the book as a child, about the East End, and then you came to live here. How did these two things play off each other?

Daniel Rubenstein: This is really the main subject we tried to explore with the children - was there a change, or are things the same? When you deal with a historic document, you are normally forced to compare it with the present, this question is unavoidable. Either things change or they are the same. For me the conclusion was quite astonishing; on the face of it, yes, things changed dramatically, people don't die on the streets, there is welfare, and people are looked after; in contrast the way Jack London describes the life of the poor people in London is really terrible.

Then you start looking from a different angle, and you see that the juxtaposition of the City and the East End remains exactly the same, the rich Aldgate Circus, the City banks, and then two miles from there the poverty of the East End; the contrast is exactly the same. When you consider the real conditions for some people, living in East London, you see people that earn only £3.10 an hour or 12-year-olds working in sweatshops. I cannot tell if their lives are better or worse, it's for them to read the book and decide. The contrast between the East End and the City is the same. There is a sense of movement, and obviously the population has changed a great deal ethnically and culturally, but

something very basic has not changed. The East End as the outlet, the exhaust of the City, this position hasn't changed.

Oreet how did you get into this idea of working with schools?

Oreet Ashery: We wrote a proposal for the project, and Morpeth School was an obvious choice, because it's sponsored by the Bankers Trust. They funded the project, we were artists-in-residence working with the school.

We took a photography slot as artist photographers, and we worked for two hours a week, for 10 weeks. We took the students through various aspects of the book. It was a multi-level project, we had an overview of what we were doing, but I don't know how far the children had the same overview; the first layer was just going through selected quotes in the book, every week we would work with a quote.

You started looking at the topography of the streets that he described; did you do this in visual terms?

Oreet Ashery: Literally on the map, as soon as he mentions Ludgate Circus, the name of a street, we asked them to find it on the map. We discovered they had no visual literacy about geography, so everything had to go back to basics. We marked on the map of the East End routes that Jack

London took. We worked with the idea of routes, Jack London's routes, then personal routes, such as walking to school, to their friends', and then arbitrary routes, like the 1970's Situationists, where you just pick a number and a letter, it's very exciting to see where you're supposed to walk. The students documented the different walks. Everyone picked letters and numbers from a hat and had their own walk. They had to explore a route that might be ridiculous to walk, but they did it, and documented it.

Daniel Rubenstein: They did that on their own, so they had to face the environment on their own. They would say 'I'm not going there, they will take the camera off me'. But it was a good experience for them to go somewhere on their own, not in a group, and to explore, just with the camera, a particular route.

Oreet Ashery: We went out with them, and they went on their own; there were different types of walks and different types of documentations and assignments. For example, we would give a sentence from Jack London and ask them to take pictures that would collide with that sentence. We also tried to make it very contemporary for them, so we had a weekend where we were taking quotes of Jack London, going to the places he mentioned. We told them to put in their own heroes as well,

and it was interesting to find that there would be black rappers - there was that kind of interaction there.

Then there was the idea of a random walk with strangers, to see how you would explore unknown territory; it might be a dangerous estate, one of them would go to a cemetery, places which are unknown and it's for them to explore. It was only within the East End, but still, in some of the places they would never walk on their own, or end up in. So that was like rediscovering the East End for them.

Another part of the project was the idea of being a stranger, the range of emotions, curiosity, fear, excitement, all the kind of things that might come up when you're a traveller, and trying to make facial expressions that would describe this range of emotions, and taking pictures of that.

And then there was street photography. We concentrated a lot on food, on what would be your daily diet, there was a lot of discussion about that, what do you like best? It was chocolate. It wasn't that different, probably, than at the time. We asked 'what would you like to eat?' - MacDonald's triple fries! Nothing changed, no culinary inspiration, no vegetables, that's not changed. And then; 'what do you think your grandmother would have eaten?'. That was interesting, they all came from different places, they imagined what they might have

Above left: 'The Spike'
Above and below: Morpeth School
students with Daniel Rubenstein at the
Tower House, Whitechapel; 'The Spike'
doss house in People of the Abyss.

eaten. We looked at cultures through food, different kinds of food culture, bagel shops, curries, Chinese. It was beginning to be interesting when we got to Halal Kentucky Fried Chicken, things started to merge and mix.

The agenda around food was a way into different cultures; we took quotes from the book, actually using the text, so they could see they could lift the text out of its context and make it relevant to them. You find yourself in a particular environment: which quote would you use for that? Just a sentence could be taken out of context and through their interpretation, become relevant to where they were. So if it's Mile End or having food in the streets, they can put it next to MacDonald's or wherever they are at the time. So that was another way of de-contextualising the text and making it their own, plus their picture to go with it.

There was a breaking point in the project; Jack London was a hero for a long time, and then discarded as a racist.

How did that come about?

Oreet Ashery: We didn't analyse the texts as such, it was a photography project really, an East End project, it wasn't a literature analysis of Jack London and the book; he was just an entry point into the East End

Daniel Rubenstein: His racist attitudes

don't show in the book, where are they?

Well, in his descriptions of the poor, for example, he is working in a particular tradition of writing about the poor that was very popular in the second half of the nineteenth century, with Greenwood and Simms. These were the urban travellers, who disguised themselves and went amongst the poor and wrote sensational type articles for newspapers of the time, and these articles were brought together and published in the form of a book. During this time, descriptions of the poor began to be racialised. In other words the poor began to be seen as, not part of the British nation, but a race apart, This drew upon racial theories, I think there is still much of that in Jack London's People of the Abyss.

Daniel Rubenstein: There is in Jack London more a kind of eugenics, a social darwinism. He does say: 'all the fit and brave went abroad to conquer Asia, India, and all the scum remained in England'. I thought of it as a sort of perverse darwinism, it is related to many things that happened in the twentieth century, but I didn't think of it as racism, because it is not so much about race as about genetics.

So there wasn't anything the kids themselves picked up on? Maybe you didn't choose those sorts of text?

Oreet Ashery: We had Frying Pan Alley

and Christ Church, where he has really gruesome descriptions of what the homeless people look like, very graphic descriptions, and you could say he is patronising there. I think they were really taking it at face value, they were just saying it is intolerable that this happened.

They took it as an accurate observation of what was really happening?

Oreet Ashery: Yes, that's after deciphering the English.

Most of the students didn't have English as a first language?

Oreet Ashery: No. I think it's not uncommon in schools in urban areas, but it wasn't a literary or historical project as such, it was more artistic. We had to use the text and make it visual, rather than an analyse the role Jack London took. But, through looking at the book, we had to become more critical. It didn't come from them, we had to make it slightly more critical, not: 'Here is this brilliant person.'

Did they see themselves as East Enders?

Oreet Ashery: No, I wouldn't say so. We had one white girl from Bosnia and one white English girl. It was interesting because the girl from Bosnia said she was from England.
I never found they had a self-conscious awareness of the East End as being different to any other area of London. We quoted things about the East End, like Jack London goes to Thomas Cook and asks them to take him there, and they say 'We can take you to Tibet but not this place where the sun never shines.' When they read that it must have evoked something, that's not my home we like it here, it's our place. But they had no particular awareness of the place or the history, apart from a strong racial awareness of themselves as being Asian, Bangladeshi, there was nothing about the East End as being different.

Daniel Rubenstein: Their local patriotism has ethnic origins.

Oreet Ashery: The East End has no meaning the way we experience it, not even as a place that different ethnic minorities inhabit. They don't see it as something like that. Not even as a touristy place where there are loads of walks and tourists come.

Daniel Rubenstein: When my parents emigrated from Russia and took me to Israel, where I grew up, I would never feel that loyal to the neighbourhood where I was living, I was still a Russian, my Russian culture was the place I belonged.

Oreet Ashery: They were extremely hot on anything racialised, anything to do with ethnic identity. When we

How was it then that they responded so enthusiastically to Jack London? What were the points of engagement?

Oreet Ashery: The idea of travelling, of an adventure. They saw him as somebody good who was telling them about the homeless, about the poor people. Their information on the social and economic situation comes from the media, but out there are homeless people and he's telling us about them, so "he's a good person."

Daniel Rubenstein: Halfway through the project we started talking about Jack London as a sort of early day rapper, and that was a good way to look at him, as this singer who comes out of nowhere and sings his song. They didn't relate to literature

photographed things, if it belonged to their language or their food culture they would be very keen to photograph that. But not about the East End as being of a particular character.

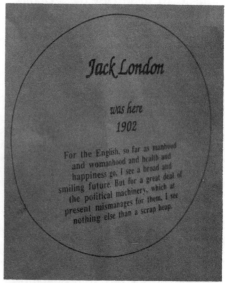

Jack London

was here
1902

For the English, so far as manhood and womanhood and health and happiness go, I see a broad and smiling future. But for a great deal of the political machinery, which at present mismanages for them, I see nothing else than a scrap heap.

Above, left and below:
Putting up plaques in Mile End.

Arty Facts

as such, they wouldn't read the book, but they related to the adventure he'd been through, and the fact that he transgressed into another dimension; that was exciting for them.

The descriptions of poverty, for me that is the least interesting aspect, but they felt very passionate about that, and they worked a lot around picturing themselves as homeless, as living on the streets. I realised that at that age it has a very strong impact.

Oreet Ashery: I really wanted to make it relevant to them, that was the concern all the time. There were seven girls, we talked about plaques, and the fact that heroes are usually men. I tried to get them to think of a woman they would like to put there, or somebody that related to them, not just Jack London. They chose another man, that was interesting, a black man, a rap singer, a controversial figure, he is a murderer, I said 'he is not a good person, he's also sexist, and you like him although he is not that good, you like his music". This way I managed to connect to Jack London.

Daniel Rubenstein: We asked the children, 'who makes history? Who decides what will be part of our collective memory and what will be gone forever?' We told them: it is in your hands now to commit something to collective memory, by placing plaques on the wall, by deciding who are your heroes and making it public. It made everyone think: 'What is our memory made of?'.

Daniel Rubenstein: It became apparent very quickly that they were not going to sit and read the book, or work on that eye to eye - so we came to the stage of tearing the book apart and giving each kid one page, and saying: chose just one sentence and work around it. Forget the narrative and use the page physically to make a collage from. We had to make the book physical to them to make them realise that there was a person there. Then when we ripped the book up they said 'Sir, you're not supposed to do that!' but they never forgot after that that there was a book there.

The story Jack London tells of East London is retold over generations. There are strong continuities between his account and some of the themes we saw in the exhibition around deprivation and poverty. The children clearly saw links there, when they walked round East London. This note of poverty and deprivation was strongly part of their perception and consciousness.

Oreet Ashery: There was quite a strong moment when we went to Christ Church - that's where he described all the homeless people - and there were homeless people sitting there drinking, and suddenly the story had come true, alive in the flesh, not just the buildings but the people as well.

Daniel Rubenstein: There is a mendicant tradition, a culture of homelessness that is 100 years old, or 500 years. But you can only become aware of that if you work with old documents like the book. What we tried to avoid was the response: 'Aren't we lucky that we aren't living in Jack London's time!'.

Oreet Ashery: The children were not homeless, they're not apparently on the breadline.

Daniel Rubenstein: They are however on a cultural breadline. These children are culturally starved, at least in the sense that they don't get any sort of official culture. That became clear when we encouraged them to talk, when we sat in a circle. It was very difficult to provoke them to group discussion, but once they started you realised these people had no heroes, they had nothing to aspire to; they don't even grow up in really deprived areas where there is still some raw energy going on and people are thinking, 'I must break out of here if I want to get a life, I don't want to be a crack dealer'. Certainly they were not going to galleries or reading books, or just meeting people and doing something interesting.

Looking back on the project, what do you
think you've learnt?

Daniel Rubenstein: For me, working in a school was a very interesting experience, I don't have anything good to say about when I was at school myself, but still I'm attracted to this environment. It is a powerful setting that can be used to bring so much good. I was trying to do a different sort of work with children, not as a teacher: to explore with them and make mistakes with them, as partners, doing art together, not education. That is something I definitely want to keep doing with children, in a school environment. I felt almost like a secret agent from a different planet. Some teachers feel very much the same. The art teachers were really wonderful, they still do an amazing job with these students.

What were your aims as far as the
children were concerned?

Oreet Ashery: Practically, in terms of photography, we covered a lot: printing, portraiture. Also, they'll always know who Jack London was, they'll have a notion of what the East End was like 100 years ago, and also the idea of re-thinking - at least they got a flavour of what went on, which is different to the usual classics that are set in exams. Through the exhibition, they saw how the work can suddenly become professional; people come and look at it, value it.

Tim Brennan was working as artist-in-residence at Camerawork and had considered Jack London's text *People of the Abyss*, but not used it in his work, when the 'East End Fictions' project developed. He says it was a 'happy coincidence' that Daniel and Oreet's proposal for a schools project overlapped with his residency. Tim has been working with the form of guided walks since 1994. He refers to these as manoeuvres; critical tours which lie somewhere between historical research, performance art and tourism.

Perhaps you can give us some sense of the occasion of the walks you are doing, and their background?

Tim Brennan: My work as an artist has come out of a long engagement with sculpture and the process of sculpture, that led me to begin making things that are generally considered to be performance art, although I just use that as a generic term. Through performance art I arrived at working with the form of a guided walk; I found that this form had several resonances, one being that it might be a way I could bridge information that might be quite illustrative of a place, but also bring in other seemingly disconnected, or dislocated, types of information. It might also allow me to pursue avenues which might be ignored in the final manifestation of artwork. Those values would then rely, in their public forms, on other discourses, such as geography or history or philology or linguistics.

So I started working with walks in 1994. I and two other artists, Dean Brannigan and Gillian Dyson set up an organisation that we called Manoeuvre, and we would produce

manoeuvres which were essentially guided walks - they were focused on London at that initial stage. This was partly born of our dissatisfaction with where one could show art work and how it was being processed; it was a kind of argument between the art world and the existing structures of curators and galleries. The idea of manoeuvring through a set of discourses, or a web of discourses, through the city, seemed very attractive. It was our first movement to what I'd call public art, but it was also very different from the public art commissions I could see around at the time. My motivation came out of an urge to be in a dialogue. I wanted a dialogic situation and not the model of the art world. That was what brought me to making walks.

One of the first walks I made was for an exhibition that was held at Camerawork, called 'Outsiders', and it was a selective artists' response to the environment. The title was from a participant conference exhibition, which was organised by Camerawork, and I was invited to be part of this show. What I did was to design and present a walk around Cable Street, entitled 'Insiders'. That Cable Street walk really did revolve around the street, it didn't necessarily appropriate what would be immediately obvious, the anti-fascist action in 1936, and focus on traditional narratives that might emerge out of Ray Walker's mural. But at the same time I wanted to make work that was very much aware of that. The walk involved deconstructing texts which could have been used for a touristic heritage mode of working on the Jewish experience of the square mile.

In order to do that I needed to replace some, not all, of those kinds of texts; what I came up with, just through looking sideways was set of bread recipes that might relate to different social groups which have inhabited the locale. So one could then have the recipe for chapati, the recipe for Irish soda bread, the recipe for Matzos, German Stollen sweet bread, English white bread. This could form a frame around which other information could be brought in, so we might be standing in front of the mural, and I could then say: This is one way of looking at things; but let's be aware of the fact that at this time, 1994, British fascists defaced the mural with a black and white paint bomb, which, in terms of its marking, looked very much like a Jackson Pollock splash mark.

Through appropriating certain art historical texts, and making the reference very current, one could talk about Jackson Pollock, his idea of the individual in his work, distilling the existentialist experience of the individual, and put that against, say, Diego Rivera's motivation to make work that is connected to a mass audience.

So that would be the kind of discussion or kind of work, or delivery in front of the Cable Street mural, and then half way through, somebody who was at the bus stop said: 'Sorry to interrupt your guided walk, but I remember when the fascists....I was there, I was at the end of the street, and I remember the day in 1936 when this happened.' I was involved in a way of working that would allow people to be involved, and it would certanly allow the passer-by to butt in.

That touches on something I was thinking about, which is the notion of space and time, and the way you handle those in these walks. It seems that space tends to dominate; does time rely on the local resident who remembers 1936 to intervene, or do you deal with time centrally?

Tim Brennan: I don't know whether this can answer the question: on that day I bought an *Evening Standard*, and I thought there might be some information in it which could be worked into the walk, and indeed there was. I remember the headline 'Mass killing in the mosque'. There had been a shooting in Israel and I found I could read this text out, making it apparent where it was from, while standing in front of Saint George in the East church. In terms of buying the daily paper and weaving it into a walk that is happening out there, perhaps this suggests that I am very much interested in a wrenching of time or a collision of times.

What about representations of labour history and East End history? It seems you don't have a model of this history having been repressed and you are simply retrieving it, like the early oral histories. Yet I wondered, for example with The 'History of the Body' walk, whether you saw it as a conscious intervention to a dominant discourse about the East End and how it has been imagined.

Tim Brennan: I don't think I could be so bold as to say it would be an intervention, because that implies that it would successfully lever apart something that is very solid, the notion of the East End as a very extensive canvas upon which members of the middle class and possibly the ruling class, have painted their own representations. Most of these representations are to do with their own projections, but in some of them there will be parts which are certainly observations. Out of that you get that repetition of underground, underclass, of the abyssal geography.

This interview can also be found on the website of the Centre for New Ethnicities Research. It was conducted as part of the centre's Cultural Goods project. For further information consult: **http://www.uel.ac.uk/faculties/socsci/culture/cner**

REVIEWS

A new literary map for Spitalfields

Debjani Chatterjee

Syed Manzurul Islam, *The Mapmakers of Spitalfields*, Peepal Tree, Leeds 1997.

The publication of this collection of seven short stories by Bangladesh-born Syed Manzurul Islam is an exciting event and Peepal Tree Press should be congratulated for bringing it out. Good short stories are difficult to write and these stories may not always be very successful, occasionally having an experimental and even unfinished air about them. But there can be little doubt that they add a fresh and distinctive voice to the contemporary British short story scene. At his best, Islam is a talented writer who impresses with his skilled craftsmanship and poetic style. These stories are wistful and nostalgic, cynical and touching, reflective and insightful of the lives of Bengali immigrants to London's East End. Located in Bangladesh and in England, the ones set in England are generally more

successful, though they always have the memories of Bangladesh, the country left behind, in the background. They combine fantasy with realism, and a dark - sometimes coarse - humour with a deft and delicate touch.

The title story, 'The Mapmakers of Spitalfields', is the best story in the collection. For this alone the book would be worth buying. It has all the ingredients of the good story: an intriguing plot with a beginning, middle and end, interesting characters, real dialogue, vivid descriptions, and the pace manages to hold the reader's attention and suspense till the very end with its surprise revelation.

The central character in the story is the enigmatic 'mapmaker' of Spitalfields, Brothero-Man, half-mad, half-holy fool, whose mission it is to walk down the streets and alleys and into the homes and shops in Spitalfields, all the while 'drawing the secret blueprint of a new city. It wasn't exactly in the likeness of our left-behind cities from the blossoms of memories. Nor did it grow entirely from the soon-to-be razed foreign cities where we travellers arrived with expectant maps in our dreams.... a strange new city, always at the crossroads, and between the cities of lost times and cities of times yet to come.'

The reader sees the colourful neighbourhood of the East End through Brothero-Man's eyes, and its businesses and its people are drawn with sympathy. 'God, how he loved the place', we are told. 'If you could fathom his mumble, you would hear him saying, *Goodly goodly delectation, look-look, dekho-dekho, such a first-class scene.*'

Bending the English tongue

Brothero-Man's language, his own unique blend of Bengali and English, is one of the fascinating things about him. Like the man himself, it is a language of adaptation. It is significant that Brothero-Man never steps foot outside his charmed 'territory' this side of Brick Lane. Munir claims that he 'can't make any sense of his babbles' which are neither Bengali nor English, but Brothero-Man has a sense of belonging, Spitalfields has made him what he is and one senses his forgiveness of Munir's moment of betrayal because he knows that Munir's words only hurt himself - it is Munir who has not yet found his place in this 'twilight' world which is Brothero-Man's natural habitat. If Brothero-Man has no home of his own, it is because he lives with, and is part of, the many inhabitants of Spitalfields: the poet who lives in a rat-infested house, the leather-jacketed cool Bengali youths, Zamshed Mia who owns the sari shop and 'never usually spent an idle moment not making a profit',

Turbanwallah from the pub, Allamuddin Khan 'the all-round guru' who has the Kama Sutra on his mind but Tagore's verses on his lips, and many other characters who might appear weird to outsiders like 'the men in white overalls' who come to catch the lunatic. But for Brothero-Man they are all members of his extended family. They too respond to him on a human level, in spite of their hypocrisies and other limitations; the pious bearded hajjis and the pool-playing youths may have little in common with each other, but they nevertheless relate to Brothero-Man in their own ways, each group recognises his special place in their community and seeks to hide and protect him from the outsiders. Allamuddin Khan argues: 'even if he is mad, what the hell they think they are up to? We have been living all our lives with so called mad people, even eating from the same plate. And certainly living in the same house and the same neighbourhood. It never bothered us. Anyway who can tell who is really mad?'

The Sonar Bangla Cafe and all the haunts that Brothero-Man frequents have that mix of East and West that is characteristic of both the area and of him. If, by the end of the story, one concludes that Brothero-Man is a schizophrenic, then it is also a schizophrenic place that he inhabits. Perhaps he has adapted to it exceptionally well and, on his own terms, he makes a lot of sense. His description of the pub holds true for his entire surroundings: 'Brothero, just like me, this place is not what it seems. You see, it's an either-neither place. But most interesting. You've to lift the veil-bhorka to see the face.'

Brothero-Man is categorised as being 'one of the pioneer jumping-ship men, who landed in the East End and lived by bending the English tongue to the umpteenth degree.' His is a link language that can communicate with many tongues in the area. The children in the playground speak his language. Brothero-Man loves listening to their rhymes: 'oh what sweet rhymes they were. Those Bengali ones, learnt from the hums and lullabies of their mothers, were mixing with the *hickory dickory dock* of those English ones.' The children who once screamed: 'Mad mad mad, there goes a stark-pagal-mad, who is madder than the hatter-mad', come to trust him and 'accept him as a permanent landmark.' But their games, their nonsense rhymes and their scream are in the same language as Brothero-Man's, who calls to them enticingly: '*Little brotheros and little sisteros, abracadabra, are you ready for Alibaba's magic-jadu show?*'

Brothero-Man is not with those who condemn Bengali youths for absorbing other cultural influences: for 'funking BAD BAD beats... hyped on Afro-man's vibes' and using martial arts to face 'the skin-headed boys in uni-jacks'. He admires them for defending Brick Lane from the 'enemy', a fight in which he too played a prominent part. He remarks: 'Brothero, do you hear what them farty-wurty mouths say? Them say how the boys have gone kaput - neither here nor there - lost in the shit-hole of a gulla-zero. What a fucking-wukking talk that is, brothero.... Sure, them don't got the brain, even the goat shit size. Aren't they everywhere, brothero, aren't these boys everywhere?'

Brothero-Man not only talks in two tongues at once ('magic-jadu', 'bawkk, bawk, bawk not knowing how to talk', etc.), but his trick of adding nonsense rhyming words for emphasis ('rubbishy-wubbishy', 'fussing-wussing', 'hish, mish, bish, I'm the king kish', etc.) is a very Bengali characteristic - an example of his 'bending the English tongue'.

When Soraya speaks in Bengali idiom to her husband, the author gives a literal translation: 'What's happened to you? Have you eaten your head or what?' In 'Fragments from the Life of the Nicest Man in Town' the Bengali lynch mob's shouts are literally translated: 'Get him, get that pig's litter, oh honest folks, get that motherfucker.' In 'The Fabled Beauty of the Jatra', a love note praises in traditional South Asian style : 'Beauty, oh my dear Beauty, you move as gracefully as an elephant.'

'Fragments from the Life of the Nicest Man in Town' is another story which I greatly enjoyed. Set in Bangladesh, it is a modern version of a well known fable about a king and his minister who choose to go mad when they realise that they are misfits in a land where everyone is insane. The traditional tale which the protagonist tells his lodger lies at the core of the story and offers the only key to understanding his strange behaviour. Also set in Bangladesh are 'The Fabled Beauty of the Jatra', 'The Ultimate Ride in a Palanquin' and some of the tales told within the story, 'Going Home'. While they evoke an exotic culture, often with nostalgia and tenderness, there is also much violence and tragedy in these stories.

'Going Home' and 'The Tower of the Orient' share some of the characters who also appear in 'The Mapmakers of Spitalfields' and, in all these stories located in the East End of London, the concept of 'home' is explored from the immigrant's point of view. 'The crossroads' is another recurring image in the book. 'Going Home' begins with: "It all began with a chance meeting at the crossroads". In 'Meeting at the Crossroads' two refugees 'from the far-flung corners of the earth', who have met as students at an English university, reach a crossroads in their relationship and in their lives as their past and future meet in collision. In fact, in one way or another, almost all of Islam's characters are at a crossroads. They all bring the baggage of their past with them, they all have dreams of the past and the future, and they all have to confront reality in the present. Soraya, for instance, in a story that is too heavy with symbolism, has to confront racism on the thirteenth floor of the Tower of the Orient, as well as her own childhood terrors, her ignorance and her ostrich head-in-the-sand tendency. When she first arrives at her new flat, she cannot face painful facts; she reassures herself that all she has to do is polish up her English to 'make friends with the neighbours, invite them round to teas and dinners.... After all, she wasn't a stranger, but only coming home.' Soraya freezes at the horror in her elderly neighbour's eyes and the hissed: 'God, what's next!' at the sudden sight of the Asian newcomers. The narrator of 'Going Home' calls London 'our city', but when an American tourist says: 'Gee! we kinda love your fog, pal', expecting to see 'the brothers of Sherlock Holmes', he knows that they have made a mistake in addressing him. He and his friends are 'the wrong sort of cousins and pals', and the tourist's exclamation: 'Holy shit! Gee! Gee!' on discovering 'only brown fellows turning away their faces in the mist', comes as no surprise. Even when the narrator falls into an open manhole, he observes matter-of-factly: 'We don't fall like Alice, because migrants like us don't fall like Alice.'

Skin-heads and tourists may not see it, but the reader senses that for Islam at least the East End of London is very much 'home'. Whoever said that home had to be a bed of roses anyway? His soul brother, Brothero-Man, 'lived by bending the English tongue to the umpteenth degree', but the author proves himself to be a fine exponent of that language.

UNIVERSITY *of*
EAST LONDON

EAST LONDON MEANS BUSINESS

At the **BUSINESS DEVELOPMENT CENTRE**
East London organisations *and their employees* can get :

- IT and INTERNET training
- access to our state-of-the-art OPEN LEARNING CENTRE :
- open 0830-2100 Mon-Fri, 0900-1700 Saturdays
- use of over 300 multi-media learning titles (video,CD-Rom etc)
- business workshops, seminars and regular Breakfast meetin
- access to an excellent Business and Management library
- access to CD-Rom and On-line Business databases
- access to video-conferencing and state-of-the-art conferencing facilities
- use of modern on-site restaurant, business "browserie", business T.V.
- special access to INTERNET BUSINESS SUPPORT sites:
    * *Business Enterprise Exchange* * *Enterprise Zone* * *"Briefs"*
- specially subsidised development programmes e.g.
        * *business start-up* *management development* * *supply-chain*

Business Partnership packages available at attractive rates
(Special Terms for Small and Medium-Sized Businesses in "Objective 2" area)

part-funded by

EUROPEAN REGIONAL
DEVELOPMENT FUND

Duncan House, High Street, Stratford, LONDON E15 2JB
FREEPHONE : 0500 007 807

development
business
centre

http://www.bee.co.uk

London Docklands
Development Corporation

EUROPEAN INITIATIVE

FLYING THE FLAG FOR LONDON EAST

A Rising in the East is occurring with a sizeable contribution from the European Union. The late 1990s will see unprecedented levels of EU funding for regional economic development in London East. The *European Initiative*, a dedicated team of policy and programme advisers based at London East Training and Enterprise Council, offers organisations:

INFORMATION AND ADVICE

- Seminars on how to access development grants from Europe

  Assistance with applications and bid writing for projects which meet the needs of the London East region

- Briefings and information tools, including *LE Journal*, the quarterly European newsletter of London East

PARTNERSHIP DEVELOPMENT

- Administration of the *East London European Forum*, chaired by Carole Tongue, Member of the European Parliament for London East and Drew Stevenson, Professor of Urban Regeneration at the University of East London

- Leadership of the Thames Gateway London Partnership's European Group adding an EU dimension to the largest economic development opportunity in Western Europe

- Establishing working relations with partners from other EU Member States

PROJECT MANAGEMENT

- Management of EU-funded projects which underpin the strategic development objectives of London East and the Thames Gateway

- Implementation of systems to control, monitor and evaluate the use of European funding in local and regional projects

For further information on how you can access the products and services of the LETEC/LDDC *European Initiative*, contact Brenda Hunt on 0171 505 2471 or Kingsley Otubushin on 0171 505 2518

RISING EAST

The aim of Rising East is to engage with the future development of East London, to give voice to its unique community and culture. It will explore the region's status as the biggest zone of regeneration in Europe and address the problems and challenges which affect the ethnically diverse population which lives and works amidst the new infrastructures.

Each issue covers a variety of connected issues, looking at social and economic trends in the area, at policy research on regional strategy and at the rich cultural and artistic life of East London.

Rising East will be published three times a year. Future topics include: analysis of particular places and organisations - the new international station at Stratford; analyses of regional trends - in health, education and household structure; comparative perspectives on urban regeneration - in Barcelona and US cities; and reviews and articles on cultural life.

Why not subscribe?
Make sure of your copy

Subscription rates, 1998 (3 issues)

INDIVIDUAL SUBSCRIPTIONS
UK   £20.00   Rest of the World £30.00

INSTITUTIONAL SUBSCRIPTIONS
UK   £50.00   Rest of the World £60.00

CORPORATE SUBSCRIPTIONS
UK   £100.00   Rest of the World £110.00

Please send me one year's subscription starting with Issue Number _____

I enclose payment of £ _____

Name _____

Address _____

_____

_____ Postcode _____

Please return this form with cheque or money order payable to *Rising East* and send to:

Rising East, c/o Lawrence & Wishart, 99A Wallis Road, London E9 5LN

CARTWRIGHT CUNNINGHAM HASELGROVE *and Co.*

Solicitors

As North East London's leading law firm, CCH & Co. offers a high-quality yet cost-effective service to handle all legal affairs, both business and personal.

- Company and business matters
- Commercial and domestic conveyancing
- Matrimonial and family law
- Personal injury and medical negligence
- Contract disputes and debt collection
- Wills, probate and trusts
- Legal Aid
- Most other legal work

Phone us or call in for immediate help and a FREE initial discussion. Cost estimates provided.

LEYTON 618 Lea Bridge Road Road Leyton E10 6AT
Telephone 0181 539 4244 0181 556 8496
WALTHAMSTOW 282/284 Hoe Street Walthamstow E17 9QD
Telephone 0181 520 1021 0181 521 8838
WOODFORD 13 The Broadway Woodford Green Essex IG18 0HL
Telephone 0181 504 8802 0181 505 4227
CHINGFORD 233A Chingford Mount Road Chingford E4 8LP
Telephone 0181 524 2878 0181 529 8368

REGULATED BY THE LAW SOCIETY IN THE CONDUCT OF INVESTMENT BUSINESS